The End of a Dream

The End of a Dream

Gael Elton Mayo

BookBlast ePublishing
LONDON

First published in 1987 by André Deutsch Limited,
105 Great Russell Street, London WC1B 3LJ.

This electronic and print-on-demand edition published in 2017 by BookBlast
ePublishing, A division of BookBlast® Ltd, P. O. Box 20184, London W10 5AU.

Mobi ISBN 978-0-9933552-9-5
Epub ISBN 978-0-9930927-6-3
Print ISBN 978-0-9930927-5-6

BookBlast® has been online since 2000 and is a registered trademark
in the UK and the US.

Visit www.bookblast.com to find out more about our clients and their books.
Scanned by BookBlast® Ltd, London.

Conversion by Mousemat Design Limited, Kent BR6 8HR.

Cover photograph: The Château de Frontenay © Gael Elton Mayo, 1958.
From the BookBlast® Archive.

Contents

Preface

Two vanishing regions of France are the Jura and Haute Provence, places that haunt. The sense of the probable disappearance of their types of people and of the traditions that formed them made me feel compelled to write this book. It is a labour of great love, for I lived in both places and would have stayed forever, but it was not so decreed.

Though the Franche Comté in the Jura may be known for its vast views, turbulent rivers and masses of wild flowers, little is generally known about its fight against the hated French, which has been described in detail only by regional historians. There is no proper written record of the two men who were the legendary seventeenth century resistants: Lacuzon and Varroz. The habits and behaviour of the *Jurassiens* in the present day, the way they are held somewhat in awe by the rest of France, may or may not be a heritage from the generations who fought such a long, gory fight to remain independent – but they are certainly a people apart. Haute Provence is entirely different, as it is also different from its well-known and faraway coast. It is secret and private, slow to be truly discovered.

There happens to be a link between these two different places. Marc Paganin, a Provençal in his late twenties whose family has been in Provence since before memory, thinks his region is being eroded by the outside world. This is also the view of an elderly *Jurassien*, a count whose castle has been in the same family for five hundred years: opposite people in age and origin, from opposite places yet their poles meet. Marc hates the suburban element that is moving in from Marseilles, Toulon, Lyon; the *Jurassien* thinks his wild land that used to be full of eccentric aristocrats and equally wild peasants with fierce habits, has been tamed.

This is the story of a castle in the Jura, of a farmhouse in Haute Provence, and of the people who lived, but failed to stay on, there. I knew four of the last generation of men in the Jura who lived in the woods in preference to houses. The castle "that looked out like a hawk over the shadows" and had been a bastion in the fearful fighting, was my home. In Provence, the feuds of two families in a hamlet under the Reissas mountain were unexpectedly human and warm – the strangeness of the nearby Drôme was another matter. . . . Here is also the tale of a young man and his dream-plan, an old man and his ghosts – and of the other men and women whose characters remain imprinted so permanently in my memory, some of whom are living there still in a sort of twilight – or perhaps simply a changing scene.

G.E.M. London 1987

Part One

The Jura

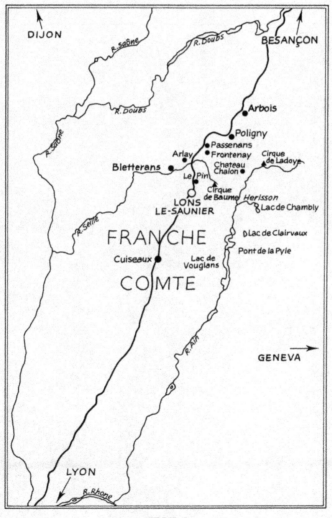

JURA

1

As recently as 1970, the Jura was a world of peasants and aristocrats, both exceedingly eccentric, and there were few social types between. Since then the middle class has grown (somewhat changing the aesthetic), peasants have become slightly *bourgeois*, but it is still a place apart. (It has only been French since the seventeenth century, after finally losing a harrowing fight that lasted through the reign of four French kings.) Europe as a whole has changed more in the years since the last war than during the hundred years previously; so be it.

When I first went to Frontenay, the peasants did not read, they did not watch television, they were "naturals" who made their own rules and were not yet instilled with desires for things they did not have; or if they had desires these were of their own invention, any outside influence would be stubbornly refuted. They were striking, earthy, gruff. They would look dour at first, but once they knew a person (which took time and meant overcoming suspicion) they were loyal.

The small group of aristocratic, educated *châtelains* were also a law unto themselves, often with curious behaviour.

The landscape is wide, with a big sky, the high pastureland breaking at times into unexpected sheer cliffs, white as old bones showing through, out of which pour waterfalls – the springs of rivers: a turbulent geological formation. The long views can seem as immense as in Spain.

I spent ten years with the *Jurassien* people, who are such a special race, living in such a special part of Europe, that it would seem worth recording their ways before the sunset fades – and while there is still time to drink the *vin jaune* and eat the *morilles* fresh from the woods in spring.

★   ★   ★

Twenty-five years ago I married a French count whose château, at Frontenay, was an ancient fortress that had been in his family for five hundred years and whose life, when he stayed there, was feudal. When I first knew him he had only recently succeeded in bringing water and electricity to his village; until then water had come from wells and fountains, also from a spring in a grotto, discovered as a miracle a hundred years earlier but not piped. Each September a Mass is still held beside this spring, to which pilgrims come from many miles.

He did not dwell in his château, but would visit often and stay a month at a time, dealing with local problems, wondering where to start restorations and living in a mess that had a certain style. The place had fallen into neglect when he was away in the war, quarrelling with de Gaulle in London; five hundred Free French had occupied it, leaving much damage. He had made a disastrous first marriage which was over, but the castle remained abandoned. It had not been properly lived in since his parents' day.

I met him at a dinner in Paris. He told me he was at a loss to know where to begin repairing Frontenay, how to arrange the place, and he asked me to stay.

He used only a few rooms. Some of the furniture was older than the usual Louis XV and XVI, it was large, heavy, Louis XIII (under whose reign the Jura was conquered by the French). Mildewed tapestries and dormice turds alternated with bunches of wild flowers. A view of seventy miles stretched from his bedroom. When he wanted breakfast he would blow a hunting horn from his window and Suzanne, the farmer's wife, would carry a tray across the lawn, which she brought to his four-poster bed and then stood gossiping; telling the latest village tales while he drank his coffee. He liked the chatter and did not need a quiet awakening.

The "service" was minimal and erratic; breakfast was the beginning and end of it, except for some soup, salad and cheese occasionally brought in for supper. He often went out to dine with friends. On my first visit we cooked dinner and wiped the dishes with damask napkins with crowns on them, which had outlasted anything practical. There were no dishcloths. Running water was still in the unfinished process of being installed – the downstairs lavatory was along an eerie passage and emptied by a trap door over the ravine. To go there required daring, it felt as if some Thing might spring from the shadows . . .

In the evenings we would sit on the terrace in an avenue of ancient stunted trees, and when twilight came, often a small wind rose, refreshing and gentle, called *la montaine*. This wind is spoken of by the historian J.E.

Jouhan (who wrote a guide book to the Jura in 1863) as a local phenomenon of summer evenings. It blows from east to west, its freshness comes from the gorge of Vaux which is cooler than the surrounding air; it arrives as the light fades.

★   ★   ★

In 1637, after generations of inherited resistance that had become a way of life, the army of the Prince de Condé took this part of the Jura for Louis XIII. Until then it had been independent, the Franche Comté (the free county) as it is still called – and had to keep fighting to remain so. It was part of Burgundy. But unlike the rest of the region which owed obeisance to the French king, the Franche Comté governed itself. When after long years and gruesome fighting it finally fell, Frontenay was under the charge of a captain called Le Flamand who was betrayed. He surrendered on a false promise that his men would not be imprisoned. When this was broken he wandered all through the castle in despair before they hung him in the courtyard – there is a belief that he wanders still. At the time of the last battle the governor (who was the *châtelain* Comte de Visemal) was away defending Bletterans against the French; he did not die at Bletterans but subsequently, in the chaos and famine that followed the conquest, of the plague. Different parts of the Jura fell at other times – the sieges went on for two hundred years before it was finally French.

The Jura is in three parts: the plain of Bresse, the foothills of the alps, and then the mountains. The Château de Frontenay is built on a prow of rock in the middle region. Seven ranges of hills fold into the view on the south side; to the west there is rolling land of vast, smooth shapes like swell on the ocean; to the east there is a walled courtyard, entered through an archway from a lower drive. Above the courtyard wall can be seen, quite close, a forest lying across the hillside like an outstretched protective arm. The only level ground is to the north, where there is a gatehouse, tall trees and the great front door. But it is the back that has the long view, facing the direction from which the enemy was likely to come. It was a look-out post, and sent smoke signals to the Château du Pin on a distant hill before a likely siege. At these times the whole village would come into the courtyard where it was the duty of the *seigneur* to defend them. Inside the walls there were stables, store rooms for grain, living quarters.

The south wall is the oldest part of the keep, built over a cliff, the sheerness of the drop disguised now by a tangle of creepers. There is a small balcony which overhangs the tops of trees which are hundreds of feet below. Looking down like a hawk into the dark shafts of shadows, or out across the seven ranges – it is like God's view; it is so old, suspended in its own static, cut off like a secret. Jackdaws circle on this side, they nest under the roof – and it is from the south, strangely, that the bad weather comes, blown up from the Rhone valley a hundred miles beyond. Seen from the small road to Ménétru-le-Vignoble, this side seems to have a face, still watching, still waiting. There is no modern world in the view from the balcony, only the Château du Pin indicates the existence of man – and of the old, forgotten medieval men who used to send smoke signals, hill crest to hill crest, and who took hundreds of years to surrender. In history this is just a period, from one date to another, but in the grit that lies under the vineyards, where Spaniards planted their grapes, tragedy lies buried.

The castle dates from pre-Roman times. No trace of this can be seen now except in the cellar, where the wall of the original structure is cut directly into the jagged rock, out of which the château appears to grow. There is a secret tunnel under the vegetable garden, discovered only fifty years ago when the gardener was digging to plant a fruit tree and his spade went through into a vaulted room, probably the remains of an eleventh century priory known to have been there. After the conquest an effort was made to build terraces and pleasure avenues, rubble was thrown anywhere – over the edge onto whatever lay below. It is thought also that the long tunnel might be an escape route, which would come up a mile away; it has been only partially excavated. One can enter the vaulted room but can only crawl along the tunnel, carrying a torch, fearing the collapse of the earth roof.

In spite of the seventeenth century panels in the dining-room, and the intention to transform the twelfth century keep into a dwelling of grace and elegance after the fighting was over, the atmosphere remains *farouche*. A strong character still dominates. The château broods. It can be unwelcoming – or bestow almost unearthly peace of spirit. It is as if the castle itself decides. Immediately on entering the hall this feeling of apartness hangs like a curtain through which one passes, leaving the world behind. It seems filled with a long, immeasurable record of feelings, fears and hopes. It is somewhere else. The independent people who lived here have left their temper, unconquered.

In other counties of France the *Jurassiens* are regarded with awe, as being different. They are thought to have strong wrath, to be *ténébreux*, like their mountains and their wild weather. (The summer storms are lurid with red or gold almost earthquake light.) I found them loyal, albeit with a certain jungle ferocity. They killed our Abyssinian cat on the pretext that she stalked the same prey as they did; in autumn, in the shooting season, they go mad and kill anything that moves; and cats are killed out of spite. The forests are not stocked and they hunt according to no proper rules, so gradually there are fewer living creatures. In spite of this fierce streak, they were unswervingly true to each other, provided friendship had been established.[1] In my husband's youth there were woodcocks in the forests, and teal, ouzel and corncrakes on the ponds of Bresse. There were grey-legged partridge – the larger red-legged ones were always rare, living in the steepest vineyards and hiding among the rocks. The boar have disappeared from the big forests long since, but this is no loss, for in the nineteenth century they used to raid the potato fields in herds of six or seven, devouring, trampling, and leaving only devastation – the people living near the woods would light bonfires at night to try to keep them away. However, today there remain snipe, hare, and still occasionally a chamois. Buzzards circle, out over the bare hills, making a mewing cry like cats.

Our woods are full of edible mushrooms: *pied de mouton, girolles, trompettes de la mort.* These last are black and look sinister, but are quite safe and make a delicious sauce. Usually they are dried and then ground into powder and kept for this purpose. In spring there are *morilles*, dark and wrinkled like tiny brains, special to the Jura, and a luxury outside the region.

At the time of Charles V of Spain the Jura was occupied by Spaniards.[2] That occupation lasted two hundred years, and the Spaniards left behind their vine stock and their method of making wine. It tastes like sherry and is unique in France; and is made still today in the very small area of vineyard surrounding the village called Château Chalon, whose name the wine bears. The *appellation d'origine contrôlée* is strict. The "château" of the

---

[1] Except, apparently, at the end of World War Two, when the *maquis* behaved ignobly, specifically in Sellières, where innocent people were denounced as collaborators in order to settle old personal scores. But those were abnormal times and long past.

[2] It belonged to the Spanish part of the Hapsburg dynasty.

village is only a pile of stones which are the remains of a tower belonging to an early king, Charles the Bald. This village was once a town with a fortress built by Charlemagne and an abbey. But already in 869 there was fighting; in 1595 the Maréchal Biron set fire to the town, and in 1637 Longueville, another French military commander, ransacked it. The raped nuns fled from the abbey. No vestiges of its great days remain, but for a beautiful small church with a roof of the old local stones called *laves*, which give a beehive appearance, some ruins on the escarpment famous for its view, and the legend that the spirit of a young girl lives in the large tree outside the church.

Certain words of pure Spanish remained scattered through the local dialect French when I first went to the Jura. They are dying out now as the outside world encroaches but are still heard among the old people; they refer to tea or a morning snack as *merienda*. My husband plays flamenco guitar like a Spaniard; he is dark like most *Jurassiens* who say they have Spanish blood. Names such as Lopez or Ramoz are common. The old people are gaunt and aloof.

It is truly another country. Even though my husband's family was also quite Parisian, he was brought up on local history and its stress on not being French. As a boy he was taken to visit the grotto of Varroz, named after the man who, with Lacuzon, was one of the *chefs de bande* of resistance to the French invaders. The cave was high up and an excellent look-out post where Lacuzon frequently camped, with a dominating view over the river Ain, above the wooden bridge called the Pont de la Pyle. There was a priest called Marquis fighting with these men – according to legend he wore a red *soutane* in order to hide the bloodstains. Wild cyclamen grew round this grotto, it was forbidden to pick them.

This view has changed however since 1960, when the valley was flooded in order to build a dam and a hydroelectric plant, submerging the bridge along with a ruined Chartreuse monastery. Today the Pont de la Pyle is of iron, it spans a great lake of an arresting green colour, the Lac de Vouglans. Smooth slabs of grey stones and wild box bushes surround it, and there is a beach where a small boat awaits passengers wishing to cruise. Though the grotto of Varroz is now engulfed below water, wild cyclamen are still protected and his name is remembered by village mayors. Jouhan called him *le fameux chef de partisans qui faisait aux français son énergique réponse. Le souvenir de cet obstiné franc-comtois est encore si présent à la population du pays qu'on rappelle souvent son mot héroique en contrefaisant son accent nasillard.* Lacuzon was even better-known, twice he took a stronghold from the French by the trick of disguising himself as a monk and persuading surrender. Cuiseaux was captured this way and is celebrated by a carving on a panel in the church, (described in Chapter 4).

The village of Frontenay is small, though according to Rousset's ency-clopaedia of the Jura (published in Lons le Saunier in 1857) there used to be many large houses, and a *formidable* avenue of lime trees leading up across a rocky shoulder to the castle's church. The farmers each have about ten cows of the breed *Taché de l'Est*, as in Switzerland. Milk used to be brought twice a day to the communal so-called *chalet*, which was not a chalet at all, but a stone house in the centre of the village – its real name was *fruitière*. These were the first co-operatives in France. The milk all went into a copper cauldron and a Comté cheese was made, weighing about 50 kilos, salted and stored in a cave in the hill rising behind the house, with a door that opened into it direct. It is best after a year and now is usually eaten too soon, unlike in Switzerland where the same type of cheese is made and old customs are still respected. A three-year cheese is best.[3] There are outlying farms at l'Écouvette, a higher part of the commune five miles away, who have their own *chalet* because the people below think (superstitiously) that their milk is acid. In fact their fields are lush and full of flowers.

There is a village in the mountains called Morbier where in former times each family owned only one cow, so they would make half a cheese at a time and cover it with soot to keep it, and the next day make another cheese which was laid on top. This gave the cheese a black line through the middle. Morbier cheese is still made, but the black line is now artificial.

When we needed milk we would fetch it in a can at the time of the *coulée*, as the milk running, or pouring, was called, which varied according to season. This was preceded by the slow amble of cows walking through the village, then later the farmers pushing their churns before them on little carts. If we arrived too late there would be no milk left until the next milking, it would have gone into the cauldron for the cheese. Two were made each day. In summer when days were long the village people would sit about

---

[3] Unlike the rubbery cheese with holes commonly thought to be *gruyère*, the true Swiss *gruyère* (Fribourg to the French) has hardly any holes and a mat surface – and the Comté of the Jura in France is the same.

under the big tree outside, gossiping. Next door there was a grocer's shop that owned the *cabine téléphonique* and was a centre for messages. It was run by a hunch-backed woman called Marthe who had a stern face like a handsome man, with dark, rather piercing eyes and a sudden smile – and so many cats it was impossible to count them; all black. The window was crammed with brilliant red geraniums. She was referred to as a sort of witch – this with affection mingled with apprehensive veneration. She knew everything that happened and was the holder of many secrets from all the telephone conversations she listened to. She had a swarthy lover of over seventy whose manliness was legendary; there was no age limit for passion. His nickname was *le costaud*, the tough one. He lived further down the hill and his wine cellar was full of bats, which could be seen hanging from the ceiling in the daytime. When Marthe died her coffin was taken to church on a red tractor piled high with flowers.

The château, with our sheep in the foreground, when wild cherries were in flower.
Rabuz' vineyard, onto which the wall fell, is beyond the cherries.
© Estate of Gael Elton Mayo

2

Suzanne and Michel are caretakers of the castle, in somewhat haphazard fashion. She comes from the plain of Bresse where it is said people are plump and easy going; he is from the mountains, with a bony face; he is eager and active, usually wearing a hat – he loves hats and owns many. Their care of the castle is certainly erratic and vague, but they tend the sheep and their great achievement is the vegetable garden, which covers the whole area below the château that lies over the priory ruins and produces every sort of lettuce, herb, more vegetables than can be told, as well as cherries, plums, pears, raspberries, currants, and old roses, zinnias and flowers for picking. Sheep dung is the only manure used and the vegetables taste like childhood memories. It is the only garden. On the terrace above there are trees and lawns, a line of clipped box and yew, an avenue of ancient hornbeam, chestnut, lime, an immense cedar of Lebanon. The garden is reached down a mossy staircase of worn grey stones; it is about an acre on a wide platform. On the far side the wall drops again to the priest's house and the lane to the church (which belonged to the *châtelain* and was given to the parish when theirs burnt down, hence its proximity to the château and distance from the village). And ahead stretches a view of seventy miles west towards Dole and Dijon in the far distance. Wherever a person may be, there is always an impressive view, sometimes portentous, sometimes peaceful, but ever striking so that a new arrival will exclaim. Even an inhabitant will not grow accustomed. Seen through tree branches, glimpsed by chance from any window, it is there. It will interrupt and impose a continual feeling of drama – a person can sometimes be disturbed by the outside element entering continually into their being.

Michel and Suzanne live in the gatehouse, a seventeenth-century stable building, built over what was formerly the defence ditch. It is a long building with an arched gateway in the middle that opens onto inside lawns in front of the château. The stable on one side of the arch has slender columns and a vaulted ceiling. The sheep sleep here – sometimes also a rather desiccated old man who Michel befriends called Firmin – and chickens perch. There is a dovecote with a roof of *laves*. On the other side of the arch is a large barn, and up above is the small abode where Michel and Suzanne live. They are still there as this book is written, living as they did over twenty years ago when I first went there, and for over thirty years before that. The people who sit at their kitchen table come and go, die, grow up or grow old – but they remain.

They keep open house, the table in their main room is always surrounded; there is only one other room, where there is a double bed and a couch in an alcove. It is surprising how many people sometimes seem to have mysteriously spent the night in these small quarters.

Nearly always there would be men sitting in the kitchen; their dark faces would be looking out of the shadows, earthy, friendly though a bit fierce, but always offering a seat. Many a time on going to leave a message or an order I would sit and drink wine or coffee with them and hear their mixture of tales and philosophy – (a similarity with Spain, where I remember in former times the old men in bars were detached from the worldly main chance). There might occasionally be a local farmer or villager, but mainly it was the woodcutter men who worked nearby, or some of the vagabonds who had no homes and preferred to live out of doors. A few of them were too wild to come in at all; one of these was Randez, who lived "somewhere in the forest", no one knew exactly where, he had his own area. He could be seen on the road at times, walking with a stick and knapsack and wearing a felt hat like a bucket; he would acknowledge a greeting, but not more. He did odd jobs across the country and would sometimes be gone for a month. I met him one day in autumn when the leaves were red like fire and the frost crackling, and in a rare moment of expansion he stopped to chat; he told me he came from the plain of Bresse, but preferred the higher land. He inspired deference. I said good day uneasily, hoping to retain some sort of balance, to stay on his good side. Usually I waved to him from across the road; he might not be a comfortable man to meet with on a dark night.

★　★　★

There was le Fritz, a name they gave to a German who had been a prisoner of war and stayed on. (The Free French who occupied the castle had strangled another German with the chain of the front door bell.) He never learned to speak proper French but invented a lingo they all understood; he had china-blue eyes and thin fair hair, he was tall and lean and always very polite. He inspired great affection in the others. He, like Randez, also took on odd jobs – an elderly hobo. He lived in a hut in the forest that he had made out of planks, with a tarpaulin roof; he had a wood-burning stove. In the spring once, walking near, I saw him picking lilies of the valley.

There was Fernand, Suzanne's cousin, who was entirely different; he earned big money and was successful in a worldly sense; he owned a huge tractor for his logs and was his own boss. Like Suzanne he came from Bresse, and had left for this higher land during the war – to escape being deported and sent to a forced labour camp. After the war, he stayed on. He bought and sold wood; he delivered all over the Jura, not just wood from our forest, but Frontenay was his headquarters. In spite of this he did not require a house of his own and slept anywhere, in Suzanne's bed preferably, though this annoyed Michel. Or he would lie on the sofa in the kitchen. He used the telephone for his messages. He was keen on women and had produced an illegitimate child in a village ten kilometres away. Apparently he had taken another man's wife and lived with her for a week in an inn; when he brought her back her husband was insulted and rather annoyed, the more so because he had returned her. "If you take her, keep her then," he said.

Fernand has brown eyes and thick curly hair; he gives the impression he would willingly take any of us to bed, he has a way of looking at a girl or a woman of any age as if summing us up, considering, but it is a friendly, conspiratorial look, impudent but kind. A good man withal who could be trusted – and he seemed always to beam with such robust health and such contentment that surely all his needs must be well fulfilled. Through the years he has grown a big belly, but otherwise he has remained unchanged; he is still there today with his red cheeks and tanned skin, the cigarette stub, the insinuating smile.

Another figure was Joseph, Suzanne's brother; enormously strong, but a simpleton and shy. He blushed and giggled like a young girl when spoken to. Like Le Fritz, he made himself a hut to live in, but his was a ramshackle wigwam affair out in the open in the middle of a vineyard. He helped with various jobs, his strength made him useful like a great machine, but he sat at the table only when there were few people – as soon as there were more than two or three, he disappeared. He did errands on his motorbike. There a consistently hot summer; normally it is acid, but drunk with relish, appreciation for its flinty taste having been acquired over the years.

Georges Roy had a domestic side; he and Chacail hailed me once from the lane and I accepted a glass of prune. Inside their house I saw socks hanging to dry in front of the fire; the oil lamp was of white porcelain with a blue stripe and a pattern of flowers. I made the strange discovery that it had been given to them by Randez (procured somehow on one of his mysterious absences?). No running water, no electricity, but logs burning and *prune* to drink, thick vegetable soup in a black pot, warm socks – and free to think whatever weird poetic thoughts filled their heads, in their meagre house. Good companions, but with no sentiment; singing or arguing, hitting each other, fighting or laughing; Chacail was the brutish one, George Roy had gentleness, except when bawdily drunk.

A deaf mute called Apollon lived nearby in a small ruined house; he was kindly, always smiling, the village people liked him and fed him. When he died they took it in turn to sit vigil by his bed all night until morning, by which time his soul would supposedly have left him. He was not fetched for burial until the following morning, when it was found that one of his feet had been eaten by a rat.

The only other house on the church lane, high above the village under the château, was lived in by the priest, who was called Grospierre; this could have been a nickname, "Gros Pierre", and suited him well, but was in fact his true surname. His house was bare but for a table, chairs, an iron bedstead – and a view that made furniture seem, in a way, unnecessary. He would get fearfully drunk and swear in Latin, "*Vada retras Satanas*" to his goats, especially the black one that followed him round; he was a farmer priest. Chickens strutted in and out of the house from the farmyard. A large white sow gave birth each year to piglets, lying in style under the slender arches of the seventeenth-century stable. Sometimes she suffocated the smaller runts, she was so large and heavy; the priest used to bet with the bishop, who came to Mass twice a year, on how many piglets she would bear. Once there were eleven and the bishop lost the bet, which he paid in champagne, but Grospierre complained it was really only *vin mousseux*.

He had true faith. The village children to whom he taught their catechism adored him; he kept bags of peanuts which he distributed everywhere, his *soutane* pockets were always filled; they were proper peanuts in their shells so he was almost always surrounded in mess. He did not bother about such things. There was the view, his faith, and his teaching. Also ideas to discuss, sometimes inspired by a shot from the *canon*. He married many young brides with large bellies – unperturbed and happy to make them lawful. The patron saint of Frontenay is, suitably, Mary Magdalen.

These three houses of the priest, Chacail and Roy, and Apollon were referred to as the *quartier bamboche*, using the Spanish word for "banquets or drunken feasts, with grotesque figures".

Grospierre was devoted to my husband, though he would reproach him amicably for hardly ever attending Mass. I once tried to discuss this interesting question with him: was it not hypocritical to go to church as a convention, an empty routine? Was it not better to go only when prepared to listen, hoping for a message from a good sermon? "Ah," he said, "your kind are dangerous, you want visions." And then, sitting in the library in the château, we discussed Catholicism. I was informed of the importance of the structure, the safety of "not questioning." My husband would tease him, "I can see your cloven hoof showing under your cassock, push it back then –" and the priest's round red face would beam and he would chuckle. They would drink a *canon* together and Grospierre would leave, after first producing a bag of peanuts for our small daughter out of the folds of his rather stained black skirts, walking off in creaky boots, a bulky figure in a beret, and like Fernand, with the eternal cigarette stub.

Half way down the hill between the two parts of the village stood a house on its own, and here lived a man called Tourez, known only by his surname. He was unsmiling and taciturn, handsome in a fearsome way: aquiline nose, thick eyebrows, virile. He was the illegitimate son of a seamstress in Passenans, the next village. He kept to himself and no one had much chat with him. One year he advertised in a newspaper in Lyon (eighty miles away) for a housekeeper. When a middle-aged-to-elderly lady arrived in answer, she discovered her duties included sleeping in his bed. They made *bon ménage* however, until she went slightly, harmlessly mad. We used to buy *marc* and white alcohol from him. This was illegal but most people made it for their own consumption, selling it only as a great favour and in confidence, for apart from the risk of being discovered there was never a great quantity.

We would sit in his kitchen tasting the various types – and once he rubbed some *quetsch* on to the back of my hand and ordered me to smell it.

were occasions in a mid-month when, out of the blue, he would drink. Where, or how, it happened was a mystery; of a sudden he could be seen riding at great speed with a scarlet face and a scowl. It was embarrassing to see him, as if he was caught in some private chasing of his unfulfilled dreams and should not be watched.

Firmin was a wanderer who lived on acorns, chicken food, and animal meal. Suzanne offered him soup but he rarely accepted; in winter he came into the stable and slept with the sheep, he was like an animal himself – a stray dog – no one knew where he came from or what he did. He was not often seen at close range – he kept himself apart – a sort of distant ghost. Only Michel could truly approach him. If sighted somewhere, by the time one reached the place he would have vanished.

★   ★   ★

There were other men we saw infrequently, as they had homes of a sort: one was Chacail, who had been in the Foreign Legion and talked of jackals, hence his dialect name. He was rather grand, because he lived in a house – it was part of a ruined farmhouse with a well outside. He had a stove for cooking and an oil lamp. He shared this with Georges Roy, a retired labourer. They both had pensions, received once a month – and they both walked sixteen kilometres to Lons le Saunier to fetch them. On the return journey Chacail stopped off everywhere, paying drinks all round. By the time he got home the entire month's pension had gone. Roy on the other hand saved his money and drank alone. He would sing, but the only song he knew was Mass, so this could be heard loud and wild, interspersed with belches, while the wine lasted. For the rest of the month they ate vegetables and dosed themselves on medicinal plants, about which Chacail had great knowledge. At the season when the plums were ripe on the tree beside the house, he made white alcohol from them.

When rumour spread that Georges Roy was ill, and his time came to die, the priest called to give him the last rites and found him under the kitchen stove. "Why is he here?" he asked Chacail – and received the tough Legionnaire's answer: "There's only one bed and he pees in it."

A month later, when he was dead, Chacail threw him out of the window. The priest observed this on his way up the lane, remonstrated again and made him dig a grave, which they did together, afterwards drinking a *canon* as a carafe of red wine is called. The local wine is good when there has been

Like buying Guerlain perfume, I thought . . . the aroma it gave evoked a morning in an orchard, bloom on the fruit and dew on drenched grass; it smelled of the very taste of the fruit. My pleasure caused him almost to smile; it was the only time I ever saw such an expression on his face. At this moment his woman appeared in the doorway with eager starlit eyes, asking if she could join us and have a taste. Her long, grey hair hung over her shoulders, she wore a short shirt to just below her waist, she had bare thighs and no knickers – an old Ophelia showing her mousey crotch. Tourez shrugged her away and she was dismissed. This rather frail lady was often seen wandering in the churchyard, making small posies of flowers – and was accused of stealing them from the graves. Since French graves have mainly plastic flowers, and the Jura is full of wild columbines, cornflowers and orchids, this was unlikely. She was accused also of stealing rabbits. They were an odd couple, living entirely alone – excluded from any village loyalties.

I used to wave to him, if he was out in the garden when I turned the corner round his house. He would always stop and lean on his spade and look to see who passed. With a slow, faintly surprised gesture, he took to waving back.

Michel and Suzanne © Estate of Gael Elton Mayo

3

Suzanne and Michel hardly ever went inside the château when we were away; it was never dusted or cleaned. The place must have seemed to Suzanne like a relic, she probably did not understand the crusade it had become to us, or the depression we had at the eternal repairs that never seemed done. She was warm and generous, but also slovenly and lazy. She had been trained as a domestic servant when my parents-in-law were alive, but she had lost the habit, sloth must have crept in, so that she did not seem to care if an antique chest was cracked or a curtain stained and streaked brown with rain, because of a window left open. Since my husband did not live there he let things take their course (fortunate to have any service at all, he said) – it was happy-go-lucky – but she would still cook well in a crisis. Her best dish is pigeon casserole with bacon and onions and many herbs; the sauce thick and brown. Young pigeons are taken from the nest before they have flown, and are therefore very tender. She taught me the proper way to make sorrel soup, which is simple. A bunch of sorrel leaves is reduced with a small amount of butter and flour in the bottom of a pan, and when (exceedingly soon) the leaves have turned to almost nothing, milk is added, and that is all. Never any salt, nor an egg, nor any of the things I have read in elaborate recipes that ruin the strong natural taste of just sorrel. The soup has such an acid tang it does not require or accept anything else. It can be made more or less thick. Sometimes I cut the long, stringy (but soft) strands with scissors to make them fine. Suzanne's blackberry jam is excellent, when she takes the trouble to pick the berries. This is natural country cooking, for in the past there was an official cook and Suzanne was only housemaid. (The old cook came to call on us one day, a tiny, wizened lady who said to me kindly, but nevertheless, "The copper pans aren't very clean, dear." I felt ashamed, then rebellious. The fifty pans hanging on the wall had been her job, with the cooking, but she had nothing else to do . . . no beds to make, no cleaning, or repairing, or wall-painting . . . or taking breakfast in bed up to friends.)

Suzanne's plump girth and serenity give a feeling of peace and inevitability; there has always been something soothing about her laziness that makes other people relax, and she is so kind, so motherly. She looks somewhat like the plump Madonna in a Venetian painting which hangs in the château. Once, when we gave a dinner party large enough to cause panic, she came to help. She wore ballet shoes and waited on table noiselessly and with perfect grace, like a sort of silent dance, one hand behind her back while the other passed the dish. (Who would have guessed, from her usual felt-slipper-garden-boot shuffle-step?) The evidence of former training was clearly visible – a revelation – and suddenly, as if a conjuror had waved a silk scarf, transparent with age, I saw the ghosts of other servants, whose mildewed livery with crowns on the buttons I had found in a cupboard. Up came *la vie de château* like a cobweb tapestry of the past.

Michel brought in a cart of logs every day when it was cold weather and stacked them beside each fireplace. It was the only form of heat. The climate is harsh. In winter we slept in gloves and ski caps, but we came in all seasons, leaving Paris at night and arriving at dawn; before the motorway was built the drive took eight hours. (Frontenay is still fifty miles after turning off the main road.)

We restored the castle together, but it was a continual fight against cracks in the wall and wood rot. When at last we found a mason to build a buttress to uphold the terrace above the vegetable garden, we had to fetch him for work as he did not turn up when promised and had no telephone – nor was he necessarily at home, but in the café drinking a *canon*, or just "out somewhere". On the oldest side of the keep, facing south, there was a large crack in the floor in front of one of the fireplaces. The anxiety this caused was heightened by the fact that the south was the bad-weather side, the wind surging up here from the Rhone valley a hundred miles away, bringing storms. An advance breeze would whine under doors – in the night the moaning could sound like a creature. The oldest wall was above the cliff, and the gap by the fireplace was in the most vulnerable place. The mason would push back his cap and scratch his head, giving forth with hopeless theories; all he could really do was cement the crack so it would not show, and what was the use of that? Yet one could not build a buttress up a cliff . . .

Ten years earlier, suddenly one morning, the outer courtyard wall on the east side had fallen into the valley with a roar like an avalanche and a torrent of stones. The farmer, Rabuz, working the vineyard up the steep slope just below, thought the end of the world had come. His two black mules reared and bolted, dragging their harness. But it was only an outer wall and after the repairs were made – although the courtyard was much reduced in size – the new wall was seen to be an improvement because it was lower and did not hide the view. The sinister crack by the fireplace was a different matter. Would the whole building slip, like the terrace that had rolled to dust that other morning, its foundation cracked by a primeval movement of the earth? The repairs became an obsession, an infatuation. To save the elephant, as we called the castle, was our life work. And always the surprises: *la mérule*, a dreaded red fungus; the roof struck by lightning; the parquet floor in the library ruckled into what seemed to be ocean waves upon our return one spring, the only time we had stayed away two months. It had been left in perfect order and was now entirely changed, making life suddenly unbearable. "It is senseless, it wasn't made for the sort of life we live in it," my husband would often say, and I would persist in believing that if only we could stay . . . "We don't live in it, that is what is wrong."

Michel and Suzanne were unperturbed. They never worried. That was the way it was. The way of *les châteaux*. Disasters were part of life. This particular time they had not actually remembered to write and tell us what had happened – probably they had not been inside the château (they rarely aired it) and so did not know the damp had got in under the floor. It was only the façade that was rooted in the ground, the test of the building was over the huge cellar; damp could not occur to them as likely – (neither as did the idea of keeping proper watch).

Once during the night there was a rumbling noise and part of the wall of the terrace above the vegetable garden subsided, rolling onto the fruit trees below. This was due to the lilac, which had twined its roots through the stones like a marching army. They could be seen sticking out everywhere like long claws pushing through the torn earth. We tried to control the lilac, clipping and pruning the shoots, realising it might invade the castle, as in *Sleeping Beauty*, but it was interlaced through crevices deep in the rock – a task for supermen. In May its voluptuous scent enveloped us, drifting in through the windows, filling the rooms – and so, like drunks who forget the danger . . . we grew bewitched.

★ ★ ★

In the Jura the storms are exceptionally violent. Windows shake and doors bang; the whole place would fill with noise. Portraits would hang crooked, the lady in the pink bonnet would look offended but still simpered, the sad-eyed grandfather with his beautiful long white hands (that had never done any manual task) would look even more wistful . . .

Out of doors the air fills with a roaring sound. Pouring rain turns forest paths into torrents, as if the very hills will slide. Branches fly about. But when the thunder rolls away a golden light spreads across the land, bringing the blurred distance back into focus, edging dandelion clocks and buttercups in copper, each leaf and grass-blade glittering with drops and the whole earth seems to tremble. Then a person would be pulled up short to wonder, might shout or sing, feel delirious with the beauty and want to stay forever, for all seasons, for always.

Sometimes on autumn mornings mist lay in the valleys in long wisps like pulled-out cotton-wool, only the crests of hills showing above it, their trees etched dark as ink so they looked like islands in a Chinese lake. The church of La Sauge, a village below, would float like a ship. When there was total fog nothing could be seen but white brilliance – we were inside a cloud – then the sun would come out from behind it, first to the high land at l'Écouvette, gradually descending in a blaze.

Good summers were as hot as Spain – white dust on the roads, people sitting in dark shade under plane trees, roses and jasmine drooping; a stillness in the afternoons. Cattle stood huddled together under trees. Bad summers made people curse, but they didn't last, the climate was full of surprise.

When the heat was muggy the snakes would come out. There were many adders, grass snakes and some vipers. Once, crossing a field of lucerne, dazzled by a reverberating storm light and wearing dark glasses, I stepped beside one and felt its coil against my bare leg, icy cold.

Peering down, then I saw the purple-and-grey skin mingling like a chameleon with the purple lucerne flowers. Another time there were two snakes copulating on the high road at l'Écouvette, in an enormous waving "O" shape. Walking with my daughter we found a small snake alone in the road, tied into a knot. It was twisting about uncomfortably – we stood there undecided, wanting to help it untie itself, but did not quite dare.

The eerie magic of the snakes is described by the *Jurassien* writer Marcel Aymé in *La Vouivre*, which tells of a simple Jura girl who held power over them and whom they obeyed.[4] The hero of the book falls in love with her after she has pursued him, then grows bewildered when he realises she is the snake goddess; he confesses to the priest that he has bedded a Satanic spirit. The strange, compelling and sad outcome when he dies (through a mistake) but she, being a goddess, cannot, and so they are separated – contains all the *Jurassien* superstitions. A café in Champagnole is called La Vouivre; she is more than local legend, to them she is a real person.

Other creatures also come out after storms: orange and black salamanders, long coal-black slugs in great quantities, and some have tiger stripes that I have never seen anywhere else.

★   ★   ★

My husband is a patriarchal figure, held in esteem by the mayor and the farmers who come to call with their problems, but this was not always the case. Before the water was piped, half the village hated him. Frontenay is divided into church-goers and anti-clericals; to the latter the *châtelain* represented the establishment, to their strong dislike.

Just after the war only the lower half of the village had water, poorly-piped by means of an old-fashioned system. The higher farms, the priest and the château were deprived – for them there was only a fountain and various wells (one of these is in a small house with a stone roof in the courtyard of the château). However there was a plan to re-build and extend the existing pipes so they could serve the whole district, and also to improve the lower system and modernise it for all. At the time of the local elections this was the great question. My husband, who had financial and technical experience through his job in the ministry in Paris, thought he could help. He asked a certain Gravier, who was head of the moderate election list, to include him on the list. Gravier, who was jealous, refused.

In a small municipality it is possible to present oneself alone, and the *châtelain* decided to do this. He spent the day before the vote visiting the entire village. There is a tradition that a glass of wine must be accepted in each house; not to do so, when it is offered, is an insult. Some of the wine was the local acid red, some was the white Spanish type that is 14 degrees. By the evening he was in great form. At the meeting in the town hall (a small building joining the school house) each candidate held forth with his

[4] Marcel Aymé is considered to be one of the greatest French writers by Jean Anouilh.

plan-to-be, should he be elected. The *châtelain*, very excited by drink, made a trumpet blast of a speech that received equally thunderous applause; those peasants who had previously not liked him, and had not even greeted him when he passed, suddenly gathered round and asked him to constitute the list of candidates and to head the list himself. He accepted, surprised, and from that time grew into the patriarch that perhaps some of his ancestors had been, for in feudal times the *seigneur* who fought for his people in a siege and risked his life to protect them had always been respected.

It took only six months for the water to be laid on – instead of a likely twenty years if it had gone through the usual stagnation of red tape that delays demands from the provinces waiting for attention from a central government in Paris, one of many dusty files.

Gravier bore a grudge for many years, until he became mayor which made him feel important – then he took to calling at the château as an equal. Indeed he came all too often, garrulous, excitable, asking for advice and yet knowing all about it already, laying down the law and talking compulsively and with pomposity.

Together he and the *châtelain* sounded like Proust's description of the *intarissable jacassement* between Monsieur de Charlus and Monsieur de Sidonie, both *monologuistes au point de ne pas souffrir aucune interruption* – each talking at the same time and not listening to what the other was saying. For the mayor, his visits to the château were a splendid outlet.

The *châtelain* © Estate of Gael Elton Mayo

4

Beyond l'Écouvette and above the high pastures there is a flat region known simply as *le plateau*. Our people never went there, though it is barely twenty kilometres away; it is spoken of as strange, it inspires no curiosity, perhaps allusion to it is even purposefully avoided. When we said one day to Suzanne, who was standing in the arch of the gatehouse as we drove out, that we were off the *plateau* (I had never been and wanted to see what it was like) she gave us a weird, wary look.

The long views from the road on the way up lead one to expect a discovery: Mont Blanc can occasionally be seen from the fields above Plasnes on a clear day. But once arriving beyond, the views seem to fade, illogically, since it is high – yet it feels enclosed.

In the centre of a village called Verges, in a walled garden, there is a château with a roof of *laves*. The village is small and consists of only a few farms. This desolate and somehow anti-climactic place is the scene of a vivid childhood memory of my husband's. He attended a party there with his father, given by the *châtelain*, Captain Chaumereau de St André, who had decided to dig up his ancestors from the village churchyard, having obtained permission to bury them in the vault of his own chapel. The party was a celebration. The coffins into which the ancestors were resettled were lying on sofas and propped on armchairs in the drawing-room, silent guests. The live ones stood about drinking champagne and eating *petit fours*. There were many people and much jollity, as if it were a quite usual feast – but there was also a pungent smell. Some of the ancestors were not long dead. My husband, who was a young boy, remembers a dreamlike feeling of unease and unreality.

The captain was impressive and well known in Lons le Saunier where he would drink in the Café du Theatre, frequented by many members of the bored aristocracy; but most of them came sedately in carriages, while this wild fellow would roar down from his eyrie on a motorbike.

On the day of our visit the château at Verges seemed derelict, the garden had tired, uncut grass and grey nettles, it looked dull, all echoes faded. The caretaker told us the family rarely came now and were selling off the furniture. "*Ils vendent le commerce*," was his odd way of putting it.

Suzanne's wary look had not been misplaced, the *plateau* was weird and depressing. Another village called La Mare had cemented in the pond that had given the village its name . . . And since it was flat land, but high, why was there no view?

We drove away and down into the wooded valley towards Champagnole, beside the river Ain, famous for its dangerous whirlpools. We decided to call on Sadi Carnot, a friend who lived at Syam, a yellow house covered in white wistaria. This house always seemed to me like part of a Stendhal novel. I loved going there – and my husband had a special affection for the man, and understanding of his "fragility", as he called it; he was witty, musical, sensitive, but given to fits of acute melancholia.

We found him sitting in the garden, and he looked at us without recognition. His wife explained that he had undergone a lobotomy and it was a great success, he was much happier now. "No more black moods, no more violence," she said.

His ancestor, Lazare Carnot had created the armies of the Republic during the revolution and had organised their victory. Because of his fame, Sadi's grandfather had been named president of France in 1887 – then assassinated by an anarchist. The Avenue Carnot in Paris is named after him. A glorious heritage . . . and the descendant sat nodding and smiling at the roses and whistling tunes to them softly – *trés musicien*. We left him in this "much happier" state, his face abruptly changing expression like a sad clown as he looked at my husband with fleeting recognition and perplexity . . . and so he remained until he died in 1985.

★   ★   ★

When we got back it was dark. We went upstairs in the gatehouse to have a glass of wine with Suzanne and Michel, like touching wood, in search of the familiar. But the bad spell continued: Suzanne was alone. She informed us that Michel had gone to fetch the priest, as he had found Firmin hanging from a tree.

Apparently a week before, Michel had come upon the old man vomiting in the stable, with burning cheeks – and so he had telephoned for the doctor. It had been arranged for Firmin to be sent to the hospital in Lons le Saunier. Later that same day, when Michel went to fetch the sheep, he had found Firmin sitting in a tree. "I am on vacation," he had said, and Michel laughed, it was a good joke; the old fellow seemed to have recovered. But the following day he was still there. "Leave me alone," he said when Michel suggested he come down, "I am going on a trip and am going by aeroplane." And in this way he had taken his leave . . .

"He wanted to remain free," said Michel when he returned. He and Suzanne calmly accepted that Firmin's time had come. It was his season, the way he wanted it. It was his right.

How can the old creature have felt about a hospital? Not that it was a warm, safe place (a thing he might well have longed for, having never had anyone to care for him) but more probably as a cage, seen with terror. Yet he had sat in the tree for several days in contemplation – comparing terrors perhaps.

★　★　★

Our sheep were brought home to sleep in the stables every night, even in summer. Sometimes Michel went to fetch them, which meant walking through the woods, up the stony track that was the old road to Geneva, only used now by the woodsmen, because the sheep grazed in the twenty acres of pasture on the high land above. Occasionally when Michel was busy, the dog was sent alone to fetch the sheep. He was a mongrel, vaguely Alsatian but with floppy terrier's ears and golden eyes. He was not a "proper" sheep dog at all, but clever. It was over a mile each way. Once there was a sick ewe who did not follow; the dog brought the herd home and then returned and sat all night with her in the field, bringing her back next morning by nipping her heels and butting her with his nose to make her go. He did not like the sheep, Michel explained. He had not taken care of the ewe out of affection, but he had a sense of duty.

This ewe died shortly afterward and Suzanne raised her lamb on bottles. Since it had not been born at the same time as the others, it could not be rubbed with one of their placentas, to give it a ewe's own smell, so there was not one who would accept it. When the lamb was half grown and the butcher called to fetch six sheep for slaughter, this favourite was included by mistake and taken away. It was the only time I ever saw Suzanne's acceptance fail. Her face was red and swollen with crying and sobs rang loud. The priest was despatched in his Citroën 2CV; he drove to Château-Chalon where the butcher lived (there was no butcher at Frontenay) and he brought it back . . . walking up the lane, carrying it in his arms, his *soutane* flying out behind, a Biblical image, a man of God carrying the lamb.

It is strange that this same man could be heard from the terrace a few days later, swearing abuse in foul language as he tramped his farmyard feeding the chickens. He had a growth under his foot that he refused to have treated; he disliked doctors. So he limped and grew angry, he called it *le gogne* – a word he spat, cursing, and it rang like a gong sound. The growth spread and invaded his leg, he became macabre; it was probably a sort of cancer for it carried him away after only a year. It was his old man's season too, Suzanne said, throwing out her hands.

That winter, le Fritz felt cold in spite of his wood stove; he abandoned his plank hut and accepted a job on a farm at l'Écouvette where he could sleep indoors. For his old age, he said. The farmer found him outside all the same, lying in the hay in the stables with their grandmother, aged seventy-five, a passionate old *Jurassienne*. True to form, there was no age limit. The hut remained in the woods and was grown over more each year with brambles until eventually it was only a strange black gap leading into a burrow.

Michel and Suzanne never had an animal put down, no matter how sick it was. When their dog had its paw crushed by a cart, they made it a splint. The wound went septic, so they rubbed it with ointment and made it a rather extraordinary boot. It hobbled, it suffered, but it lived. They collected stray animals – once a dog they said was half fox and came from the forest. The dogs lasted until they grew grey-muzzled and deaf, only the cats disappeared, shot by the local people in the autumn.

One summer the vet in the village told me to be careful in the woods, as there was a wave of rabies. How could one be careful? "Take a stick with you," he said, "and warn any children who may be staying." A stick in the face of a foaming beast? But no, he explained, rabies causes a character change – a nice domestic dog might become fierce, and the contrary could happen to a fox; he might approach looking friendly, wanting to be fondled perhaps. A child would be delighted.

A man who lived near the forest had been bitten by a dog who was known to roam and have fights; because of this the man was having rabies shots, one every day for twenty-four days. He was sick, depressed and in anguish, partly from fear and partly as a result of the treatment, which causes total upset. In the end the suspected dog did not develop rabies so the man had suffered for nothing – but had he caught the disease he would have died.

There was no other mishap; but one evening in the autumn a fox came up the stairs in the gatehouse, looking friendly, Suzanne said, but also looking peculiar. She closed the door on him and shouted to Michel through the window to get his gun.

★   ★   ★

Arbois is a small town fifteen miles away where there is a chef, Monsieur Jeunet, who cooks only Franc-Comtois dishes: chicken with *morilles* in cream and *vin jaune*, pike soufflé, rabbit roasted with tarragon, a "blood omelette" as it is called, which is made with hare's liver. He says the Jura was so often invaded by outsiders who left their cuisine behind that he tries to keep the old truly regional dishes from dying out. "It took thousands of years to perfect the cooking," he laments, "and only the last twenty to destroy it – even our invaders' recipes are fading . . ."[5]

His restaurant is rather unsuitably called Le Paris. He runs it with his sons. Indeed, to say that Arbois was often invaded is an understatement. It was besieged in 1478, 1538, 1595, 1674 . . . always defended with great bravery (*"une intrépidite sans égal,"* recounts Jouhan). After the 1595 siege, Henri IV looted it and seized the wine, leaving hate and scars behind. The commander of the *Arboisiens* was hung on a lime tree, which lasted as a landmark until 1836. Nothing is left now of the ramparts that originally surrounded the town, their upkeep having been the main expense and endeavour of the people, except for a tower called the "Gloriette". They probably still feel they are a people apart, but it is peaceful enough, lying along the river Cuisance – the houses have overhanging balconies full of flowers. There are many tourists in summer – and there is a large house where Pasteur spent his youth and made some of his most famous experiments.

The region is full of these delightful small towns, such as Poligny with the fifteenth-century church of Ste Hippolyte (a bas-relief of this saint

---

[5] Monsieur Jeunet has become quite famous, to the point even of being on English television.

being quartered hangs above a tall figure of Christ) and carved wooden Renaissance doors; and Lons le Saunier where in 1760 Rouget de Lisle, who wrote the *Marseillaise*, was born. There is a plaque to him in the rue du Commerce, where the arcaded houses have a very Spanish feeling. Here there is also one of the most famous *patisseries* in all France: Pelen, Prince d'Orange. They make a dark chocolate cake, a coffee cake called "la Japonaise", a *praliné* cake with a squirrel drawn in fine sugar and ground hazel nuts on the top, and a green cake that tastes like clouds, it is so light, impossible to guess what it is made of – in fact a very light *crème de kirsch* and almond paste – among countless other specialities.

The "Côtes du Jura" wine drunk with such relish by the priest and the local people is made from three types of grape: *Poulsard*, which has an oval shape and not much taste but good body; *Gamay*, red and strong; and *Enfariné*, so called because the skin is whitish and looks as if it has been dipped in flour. The advantage of this last grape is that birds do not like it. (To put birds off vineyards there are sometimes *murgers*, a mixture of hedge and stone wall, the hedge part being made of this grape.) There are three sorts of *Gamay*, the white, known as *melon*, the red, and the very red, called *teinturier*.

The *vin de paille*, literally straw wine, takes its name from the grapes formerly being laid out on straw to dry. When it was found that they were too often eaten by rats and mice, or mildewed, they were hung under the eaves instead. They are dried for one-and-a-half months, then pressed. The juice is very sweet and makes much sugar when fermenting in the barrel. It is a dessert wine.

Château-Chalon wine is made from *Savagnin* grapes. These are not good to eat, being small and hard, but are rich in tanin. Their name comes from the blue clay in a geological streak across the very steep slopes of the small region surrounding only three villages, Château-Chalon, Ménétru-le-Vignoble and Névy-sur-Seille. The wine must be kept in oak barrels to reach maturity. It renders only a small amount and the tanin takes five years to oxydise, which is why it is so expensive. It is white wine at the start but turns a darker, richer colour, hence the name yellow wine.

A geological phenomenon of the Jura are the many *cirques*, as they are called (or in Jouhan's language *grandiose hemicycles*): cliffs that drop suddenly from pastureland into valleys as much as five hundred metres below, forming great semi-circular walls of white stone. Near Névy-sur-Seille there are grottos where the villagers would hide during the many wars. During the Terror, Mass was celebrated in one of these caves; Lacuzon is also known to have hidden there. Baume-les-Messieurs, where Irish monks founded a monastery in the sixth century, is below the source of the river Seille. Here a high cirque shuts off the end of the valley, and inside it is the spring. Before cascading out into the light, this small but turbulent river runs through a series of tunnels and caverns which have local names: the bat's room, the paradise room and – the favourite, so glimmering it is as if "lined with diamonds" – Cleopatra's boudoir. In a small subterranean lake blind shrimps are to be found, the subject of a study by the biologist Armand Viré. It is possible to visit this underground world, walking on narrow bridges and holding an iron hand rail. Stalactites, stalagmites, a deafening noise of rushing water . . . it is a magic place but eerie, and gives a feeling of giddyness – even, in the bat's room, of ghoulishness, for these creatures hang down in black garlands, making a noise like a thin violin heard through the water sound; it is recommended "not to disturb them or they would fly about like spectres". Only after the river pours out into the open (its fall referred to as "Little Niagara") does it become peaceful, with rapids flowing over smooth grey stones, green pools and trout.[6]

Farther away, towards the alps, there are more than a dozen large lakes, some much frequented in summer, others hidden in forests, and secretive. Around their shores flints and bronze relics have been found, also arrowheads and jade ornaments, which indicate an ancient civilisation of lake-dwellers.

★ ★ ★

To name some other *Jurassien* towns, there is Dole where the bell tower of the church can be seen from miles away – before the town was conquered by the French it was called "the lighthouse of liberty". The parliament of the Franche Comté was originally here, but after Dole capitulated, following a siege during which the bell-tower received "a thousand canon shots", it was removed to Besançon in spite of a declaration by Louis XIV that he would respect an agreement to leave it where it was. Dole also lost its university, which had been founded in the thirteenth century. After its defeat the town, which used to be called "*la Joyeuse*", was called "*la*

---

[6] Inside, the grotto has now somewhat changed. Details are in chapter 13.

Dolente". But today it is not a sad place. It bustles with activity and there is much to see: old Spanish houses dating from the occupation; mediaeval streets; fifteenth-century manuscripts in the library; a superb wrought-iron grid in the church of St Jean. It has, too, good cafés, restaurants and shops.

Then there is Besançon, called by Victor Hugo "the old Spanish city", a town with a famous theatre and an important provincial life, with a history that goes back to 415, when it was sacked by Attila. In the Second World War Englishwomen were interned in the citadel high on its hill, the great Fort de Vauban. There is an interesting exhibition here of the Resistance, including photographs of *passeurs* who smuggled people across the German lines into the free zone.

Ornans is a small town on the river Loue where the painter Courbet was born. It is called Little Venice because the houses overhang the river – there is always fresh trout on the menu at the Hôtel de France.

Cuiseaux is a village worthy of mention, for it was captured in 1636 by Lacuzon by the ruse of disguising himself as a Capuchin friar. In 1477 the armies of Louis XI had already set fire to this town (as it then was), it had known religious wars, the plague in 1584, so by the time Lacuzon's, battle was over "only four towers were left of the thirty-six in the fortified walls," according to Jouhan and another *Jurassien* writer, Louis Lautrey. Today ruins of one lone tower remain in the wall near the cemetery, and inside the church (outwardly restored in the nineteenth century but old within) is the carving that immortalises Lacuzon. It is small and hard to find: at the end of the choir pews, close to the wall, there is a fox in a pulpit, with a rosary over one paw, preaching to some hens who are too foolish to notice that there is a chicken in the monk's hood on his back. I enquired first about this carving at the town hall where the deputy mayor was "not interested in churchery". However the priest directed me to the exact place.

It is a paradox that the Spanish, often thought of as a cruel people because of their Inquisition, have left behind them an atmosphere of civilisation, while the French, famous for their civilisation, have left behind memories of looting, rape and death.

From Frontenay I used often to look across at the ruined château of Arlay on its hill. It used to seem especially haunted and somehow draw closer at sunset, with its remaining wall and windows like worn eye-sockets submerged in dark green foliage – but at all times it had the creepiness of an old tapestry.

Arlay today is a long, straggling village, but it was formerly a big town in three parts: the upper part was a fortress, the middle was the district where doctors, scribes and merchants had their dwellings, and a lower quarter lay along the river. When allowed to live in peace it was prosperous, and famed for its painted linens, leather goods and tools. The people were valiant and somewhat wild – they fed their pigs on horse meat – but they were governed by an intriguingly modern and progressive first baron, Jean of Chalon-Arlay. In 1276 he drew up a plan for them: any foreigner of any religion might come to live in Arlay, provided he accepted the code of behaviour which decreed that there should be no thieves, no murderers, no violence, no outsiders brought in without permission, no fornication – but this last had to be witnessed by two persons not of the family, and the culprits must be caught *culottes basses* and not just by hearsay. Crimes were punished only by fines. Unfortunately the rule of the first baron, known as *le sage*, finally gave way to a horde of "wizards and forgers" who moved in to the lower town, and the quarter along the river became known as "*la Diablerie*".

Arlay was not destined to know much peace. In addition to fire and flood, a dread epidemic among its cattle called *épizote*, and the plague in 1349, 1481, 1630 and 1636, it had to contend with the French – for under the French kings the town was repeatedly pillaged, looted and set on fire. In 1479 Louis XI's General Craon had first destroyed most of the château's keep, its chapel, its storerooms and its prisons, after taking it by night from the eighty-year-old military commander Aymar de Boujailles who had previously fought off three attacks. De Boujailles was hanged. Then Craon had the *châtelain* of Arlay beheaded in front of his own château. It was d'Aussonville, for King Henri IV, who in 1595 demolished the watchtower of Chantemerle on the outskirts of the fortifications, then demanded of the town such an exorbitant ransom that all the jewels of all the women were not enough, whereupon he took hostages, whom he then garrotted. It was in 1637 that General de Longueville finally burned down most of the remaining upper town which surrounded the château – the bourg-le-haut. Finally – Arlay surrendered to Louis XIV in 1668.

In 1773, a century after the chaos was over, the Princess de Lauragais built the present house (now called the château) and a monastery on the land below the ruined keep; she made a landscaped garden on the hill with arbours and avenues of trees. There must have been a period of elegant promenades, for there are notices in white enamel pointing to the whereabouts of lost sights, and there are the remains of a chapel and of a town bakery called *le four banal.* Today these notices have chipped, rusty edges and more recent placards say: "Danger, falling stones". The trees have grown enormous and create a murky gloom that hangs like the shadow of the past, in spite of beauty. There are few visitors now. Inside its park and run-wild gardens it does not even seem haunted (there would have to be so many ghosts, beheaded *châtelain*, strangled women, hanged commander . . . torture instruments were found when the monastery was built), but it seems very still, with a desolate, unearthly quiet.

★ ★ ★

Perhaps the lasting impression in the Jura of "good Spaniards", so different from the French, is due to the fact that the Spaniards never wanted the Franche-Comté for its own sake. Their route through Europe to their Flemish possessions passed through it – free passage was a strategic necessity – that was the reason for their presence. But they held it for two hundred years and their occupation forces had to live there, and so they built themselves houses and made themselves sherry. Their pleasant habits of living were not forced on people but implanted by chance, and over a long time.

The French came with a deliberate objective. Again and again they attacked in frustrated fury because this was the territory that the kings of France needed and coveted. In books of general history the way that the Franche-Comté was captured and finally brought in to France in 1674 is usually passed over with little detail, but regional accounts give lurid descriptions of brutality and bloodshed.

One writer, describing life in the town of Salins, calls the year 1639 *la plus funeste.* After fire, pillaging and the plague came famine. A few families with money took refuge in Switzerland; these were the fortunate, the mass of people starved – most of their homes were charred ruins. A soldier whose hand had been crushed had to have it amputated; the surgeon asked if he could keep the hand in payment, and when his request was granted, he ate it.

And so the *Jurassiens* fought incessantly through the years, each generation inheriting this struggle. Perhaps this is why they are known as *ténébreux.* My husband's vendettas have been fearsome. His sons by his first wife refuse to see him. The Jeanneret family, whose farms at l'Écouvette are quite close to each other, have not spoken for twenty years because of some ancient betrayal. Though the loyalties of the Franc-Comtois are admirable, their hatreds are like the Jura's torrential storms, or the whirlpools in the river Ain (where many have drowned), and they are strange, like the hellebore (a witches' cure for madness) which grows wild in quantities not seen anywhere else.

The conquest was long ago. But the present is born of the past, and it is ironical that although the Jura has long been a part of France, its people remain somewhat inaccessible, and the visitor to the towns with arcaded streets, and houses built round enclosed courtyards, will still feel the Spaniard.

★   ★   ★

There were many friends. The Comte de Merona lived in a village of the same name, retired from the world. He hardly ever went to see people, only out to tend to his farm and his sheep. He was an intellectual with a superb library – a solitary person. His wife had abandoned him and the countryside in the early years of their marriage for a frivolous life in Paris. The Comte d'Étampes, a late friend of my husband's, had lived at Pierre-en-Bresse, and was almost penniless. He made his abode in the stable of his glorious but derelict château, Louis XIII brick-and-stone. He was pious, humble, went to Mass every day. During the war, as his home was near the demarcation line, he sheltered and hid many resistants. When the Gestapo found out, he had to flee. He returned after the war was over and found that the villagers had tended his sheep, cut the hay, looked after his land in loyalty. He acquired a moped for the new life he was starting to be able to live, but was killed on his first ride on the road outside his front gate.

Laurent Monnier was a heavy-set, worldly man, a *bon vivant*, tall, with great presence. His grandfather had built an iron smelting factory in the period when factories were small brick buildings with a certain grace, and their owners lived nearby. This factory had closed, but Laurent lived in the great house next door which had its own chapel and a large garden and park. In front of the house there is a fountain with two black iron swans, wrought in his forge. (In the château we had some very small, thick, black iron pans the size of one egg. These were made in his factory, especially for use on a wood-burning stove; an egg cooked this way tastes like no other.) The wallpaper in his drawing room was bought in the Paris exhibition of 1880; each wall has one enormous bouquet of flowers, and the effect is very romantic. Monnier died in 1980, an old man, but a lavish host until the end, giving large dinner parties with succulent food and brilliant conversation. His house, like his heart, was open.

His life in the provinces could almost have been in another land and another century – yet he was also well known in Paris, sculpted by the Russian Chana Orloff (who died in 1968 and whose busts are in the Modern Art Museum). A frequent guest at his table was Youla, an old lady who had lived in Russia and now spent her summers in a peasant's cottage beside the convent of Voiteur, with a garden full of flowers.

On the road to visit these friends lay a half-forsaken village, St Lothain, where the church is a sturdy, primitive building in which, in the seventh century crypt below, are the relics of its saint. St Lothain died in 574. He lived a solitary life and shunned the world, but in spite of this, miracles took place, because, "God wished to show his pleasure". A person sitting in this church can feel the old centuries in the complete silence. The steeple has an onion tower; there are many of these, their origin and slightly Byzantine appearance unexplained.

As the years passed I grew ever more deeply enclosed in this "other country", with only a rare echo of Paris.

The château seen from the vegetable garden © Estate of Gael Elton Mayo

5

Our attic contained a mixture of treasures and junk. Old grey corsets and broken chairs – a gold bed carefully covered and wrapped in hessian, discovered when I noticed a gold artichoke from the bedhead poking out of a hole in the cloth. A rusty cockerel full of bullet holes: the weathervane of the church, found in the vegetable garden by my husband's grandfather (the bullet holes date from the 1870 Franco-Prussian war). A doll's outfit in a small trunk, with a list of her clothes carefully written out – in whose hand? Most of them are still there, dusty, tender, but their owner gone. Where is the doll now who had such parasols and wore such tiny, handmade kid gloves, and went away leaving her things behind? She also has a nurse's uniform dating from the Great War, so she was a patriotic doll-lady who did good works. Fur muffs in round boxes, and a fan . . . This was the past, but the present seemed to be made of the same stuff and to hang in the air like specks of dust in the shafts of light. Ferreting about in the attic one lived inside a tenseless space – under the huge roof with its fifteenth century beams and their wooden pegs. When the wind rose it seemed to sway and move slightly, creaking its timbers like a ship.

A longing started to grow: to be able to live all the time in the Jura, with the ruffians and peasants, the few well-read friends and the immensity of the land, the small familiar villages, instead of visiting it for mere holiday periods, our time spent on repairs that had to be continually re-done. Each time we went away, leaving the château in order and beautiful, I looked back at it in anxiety wondering what new surprise it would spring on us at our return. As if it was angry.

It needed us, it needed care.

I studied ways of achieving an equivalent to my husband's salary (he was Inspector General at the Ministry of Construction). At least five hundred sheep would be required, and there was not enough land. We had 150 acres of forest but only twenty of pasture. (Before the revolution, and the gambling debts of one of the ancestors, there had been 4,000 acres.) Tamworth pigs? They could live in woods. Or could we bulldoze part of the wood and make more grazing?

In the search to acquire more land I drove about, as far away as Orgelet, but there were too many smallholders. Mink? We visited a farm: they are vicious and bite the hand of the keeper who feeds them and cleans their cages, so that he must wear strong gloves. They like their meat rotten. On the day of our visit it was hanging putrid from the roof of their cages. We agreed that to breed them would be too repulsive a way of life. A retired admiral grew rhubarb as a crop and sold it to jam factories; it does not freeze in winter. Could we perhaps bottle water from the spring in the grotto? It was as good as Evian or Vittel. We had sheep, and we had caves, (the secret tunnel) so could we not make Roquefort cheese, which is ewe milk matured in a cavern? Or grow mushrooms as a crop, since they are grown in caves?

"This is not serious," my husband said in alarm at all the ideas. He was right, they were not convincing, they were dreams, perhaps for another type of man, for he was not a gambler. The castle must have put a spell on me and wished me to stay, a useful worker for its cause. But also he loved his Paris life, he was not entirely a countryman, though he took pleasure in his woods and could imitate the screech of the blue jay so well that the birds answered, echoing through the trees. Sometimes it was hard to tell which was which.

Every three years we would sell our wood. It was used for parquet floors, furniture and fuel. In the last fifteen years this commerce has almost entirely ceased; fuel is now oil and furniture is made of pine or chromium. Our trees were hardwood, beech and oak with some acacia (used for stakes in the vineyards, now these are of iron), some elm and poplar, and a very few pine and fir.

The men who came to buy would stamp about the forest smoking cigars, like gruff antique dealers, while my husband marked the trees of their choice. (The forest was never cleared, it was cut in a ratio of one tree in seven, letting others grow, and planting new ones.) Then they would come indoors and sit round the dining-room table, each one placing a sealed envelope with his offer in front of his place. My husband would read them in turn and take the highest bid. The sale was then agreed with some *vin jaune* or *vin de l'Etoile*, and much wild, raucous conversation.

I took to staying behind in the château when my husband had to go back to his job in Paris, I was tied by some sort of pledge, or maybe a fixation. Yet it was often creepy there alone. At times I was frightened at night and would lock the door of my room but still expect it to open – slowly perhaps – with an invisible hand. At other times there was almost celestial peace, removed from earthly noise and haste – in a detachment like a spiritual levitation. Then I would walk all over the building at any hour. (If I met a ghost, it could well be Le Flamand, and would be interesting. To have such a name he must have been an outsider, and so was fighting for an ideal in a cause . . . ?) Sometimes, returning from the garden I would stand in the hall on the worn mosaic floor with the lion and the two stars and the crown, and look at all the doors opening into it, and up at the high ceiling, and wonder about the people who had loved it and fought so hard to remain free. Who had carved the wooden staircase with the boar hunt? At the bottom steps there were tree trunks, men with spears and dogs; as it reached the middle there was the boar himself, and by the upper landing there were crows in high branches. It had been built when the facade was heightened to a second storey after the fighting was over. The artisan carpenter who carried out the order must have loved his work. Quite different was the spiral stone stair with its worn hollow steps, in the tower, leading to the oldest rooms and above them again to the attic. A white owl lived at the top of the tower and left rather human-looking turds on the steps, so I would wonder if a tramp could be hiding and feel apprehensive again. Fear could return suddenly, when not expected, from a chance thing.

Once or twice at first, when I was afraid, Michel came and slept in the room next to the kitchen. But I knew I must overcome the fear, since it was to be "home".

Suzanne said nothing would induce her to sleep in the castle alone, especially on the "old side". In the marshy plain of Bresse where she and her brother had lived as children, she told me they were instructed not to go out after twilight, "because of green ladies".

The jackdaws flew only over the old side which could sometimes be creepy.

6

There are those who believe in ghosts and those who do not. I record some facts, certain things that happened, with no embroidery.

One summer when we were expecting a large number of guests I went on ahead with a Portuguese maid to prepare. She brought in breakfast one morning and asked what it was that I had needed in the night; she slept in the room next to the kitchen and had heard me walking round the table. But I had not been there, and had slept especially well, not waking once . . .

"I heard you come in," she insisted, "I called out and you did not answer . . ." and as she spoke I saw her face change as realization came: it had not been me in the kitchen. Before this she had slept with her door open, she had known no fear and was not given to imaginings.

What exactly had she heard, I asked, after receiving no answer from whoever she thought was me? A person had walked about, and then gone up the stairs – she added reflectively that they had a heavy tread, as someone might in strong shoes, or men's boots . . . and the more she remembered the paler she grew.

"I would have had bare feet, or ballerinas," I said, unintentionally making it worse.

Her eyes grew like deep pools. Who, then? She refused after that to sleep by the kitchen and moved to the room beside mine, leaving the communicating door open. We fetched Michel and did the rounds with him, in case a prowler might be hiding. We found no trace, though in the attic Michel picked up an axe that was lying on the floor, saying it had been missing a long while, it was the best wood chopper and he was glad to find it. I was horrified; at the time I was writing a novel in which a maniac was hiding in the attic and planned to use an axe to kill.[7] It was unreal. I tried to tell Michel and Suzanne later of the fearsome idea that my novel might

[7] *It's Locked In With You.* Hutchinson, 1968.

come true, but they did not comprehend, and there was never an explanation of the steps.

Another summer my sister Patricia came to stay. We were sitting in the kitchen one afternoon alone (there was no help that year) and talking of all that was being done to the château; my sister asked casually what would happen later, who would inherit. It had always been handed down through the women, changing name four times in five hundred years by marriage, but never changing blood. She asked if it would go to the sons by the first marriage, or whether, as by tradition, it would be through our daughter. When she pronounced the child's name there was a violent stamping, scuffling and running of feet in the room overhead (my bedroom). It sounded like a person. We paid no attention at first – it could have been Michel delivering wood – but then on second thoughts, something struck us both; it was not his time of day, nor would he come when the baby was asleep. We went upstairs and looked everywhere. There was no one.

At night once when my husband was in bed, running feet stopped abruptly outside his closed door. They were loud and distinct enough to wake him immediately from a deep sleep. He got up mechanically, thinking it might be Michel on some urgency, and went to see what was up. When he found no one at the door, and the passage empty he went downstairs to search. There was no one anywhere.

One summer we brought a Hindu cook, and went away for ten days to Italy leaving him behind. He was the only person who ever, apart from myself, stayed in the castle quite alone; he said he did not mind and would like the holiday. On our return I asked how it had been. "Very splendid on the whole," he said, and told how he had heard lovely music. I asked what sort of music, thinking that if it had been his dream it would probably be Indian. But he described it firmly as "European music". It came from the drawing room where there was a grand piano, but he had also heard string instruments. This he had enjoyed, but what he had liked less was the figure of a very tall man standing by his bed one night and asking what he was doing there. "A racist ghost, Radha-Krishna?" but the joke was not funny, this was the bad part, he had been terrified. The man went away, but he glimpsed him another time at the end of the long passage on the "old side". He was the only person who ever actually saw anything.

These events I have recounted were infrequent, though impressive they were spread out over many years. However what happened often was a feeling of presence – an atmosphere that someone or something was there. This was very strong, as if it could breathe, was alive. The actual events, when something more specific took place had a similarity: they all happened during an everyday afternoon or evening, and in each case were thought at first to be merely some banal human activity. Only afterwards, when there was no explanation, people would register bewilderment, puzzlement, and with the realization came shock – fear would creep up the shins.

★   ★   ★

To recount the incidents of atmosphere: on one of my sister's visits she came with her husband who brought his son of eighteen with him. The boy was so frightened that he took the mattress from his bed and slept outside the door of their bedroom. Yet he was fearless. He later won a gold star in Australia for rodeo riding, he would ski across a narrow ledge, he would brave a bull.

A Spaniard aged twenty came as *au pair*. He would never stay indoors after dark if there was no one else about. At the end of that summer there were no guests; in September the light fades early – if we were out and did not get back till five o'clock, not yet dark but growing dusky, we would find him strolling on the lawn, but never indoors.

My two older children, Guislaine and Stephen came to stay at a time when I was quite alone, before the baby was born. On this occasion there was no special event, but we simply felt we were never by ourselves, to a degree that my son (especially) found shattering. Someone – or something – was in the next room, or the passage, or behind the door. In an ancient place it is easy to have the creeps. But not with the sunlight on the terrace outside the dining room, where we sat laughing and talking in the tremendous fun of being all together, for it was a family reunion. Guislaine knew the château, she had been with me on my first visit, but then had gone away to America where she had a job. Stephen had never seen it, he also lived in America. They were both on holiday; he was twenty-one, she was seventeen – the visit was one of excitement and pleasure. There were languid summer afternoons with a smell of box hedge, lizards on the wall – the terrace where we sat was on the western side with the rolling view towards Dijon, crests of hills in far distance, like small purple lions – it was a safe, reassuring view, not like the one from the small back terrace which was dramatic and could be disturbing. There was nothing but peace . . . and yet. . . . What was that? Who is there in the dining room behind us? My son refused to go upstairs alone, even in daylight.

At the weekend my husband was due. We went to meet his train at Poligny, leaving before dark, glad to get away. We had dinner in a restaurant. "If he isn't on the train," my son said, "I'm not going back there." We joked, we drank the local red wine that was exceptional that year, but truly he meant it. Fortunately my husband had not missed his train. We returned all together and once the master had come the tension was partially broken – but it came in cycles anyway. (On what did it depend?)

The next day it chose to start a new cycle, entirely different, spreading its magic and peace. Then my son so loved the place that he said he would come back one day when he got married, for his honeymoon. (As, in fact, he did.)

The road to Ménétru-le-vignoble, and the lower village, seen from the battlements.

© Estate of Gael Elton Mayo

7

When the summers were over and the guests had gone, I stayed on, working at repairs, mending and painting but also just reading and walking in the forest where I knew every tree, with my Abyssinian cat following. There was a hollow that was especially good for *girolles*; these came when the leaves were turning yellow – in the fog the trees would glow like lanterns and radiate a gold light. Inside the château at times I would talk outright to the "presence", when it was there. ("Why should you mind me? You weren't French – I am no more foreign than you and am repairing the place you loved, so you should be pleased and make me feel I belong.") I lived in a state that alternated between awe and serenity, never boredom. Ecstatic uplift or fearful unease ... once or twice, even terror. But with the first light of daybreak, there would be an immense peace, unlike any other. Either way, when the time came to leave I could not bear to go. The fear did not matter, I was training myself to overcome it, like learning a philosophy, or perhaps a language. There were rules, logical arguments and answers to have with oneself, like a remedy for a snake bite. Because it could still come in the sudden way it had, with no warning ... nor reason. ... Shafts of red sunset light coming through the windows of the room with the parrot wallpaper ... Entering the room singing, to fetch a book – and stopping short: I was not wanted. The room was in a different tense, I was in the present and had entered someone's past. So I would retreat. But not always, for I would try to master it, and would argue: if you are still here, *you* are in *my* present. You lost the battle, but not the château, because it is still yours ... but it is mine too, and I am fighting to uphold it, not to let it slide down the cliff ... Help me then.

And so it grew addictive. And I won, because I learned to cope. There came a time when if there were creaking sounds at night I was no longer afraid, and knew it was just the "elephant" settling into his carcass. It was home. Nirvana. I would go to bed and sleep the deepest cotton wool sleep ... In

lambing season there would be bleating in the stables through the night –
sometimes Michel's lantern could be seen swinging as he went to attend the
ewes. Owls would hoot. When the nightjars made their churring shriek, it
meant the weather would change. Sometimes in summer a bat would fly in
and out again, a creature of such complete silence, no wonder they were taken
for spirits. In spring the whole room smelled of lilac. The seasons passed and
returned. Time was marked by the angelus ringing at 7 a.m. and 7 p.m. – and
because the church was just below the walls the sound was very close, it was
round and loud, rolling like hoops through the stone building with deep, clear
acoustic, up the spiral stair, filling the attic roof, out again and down all the
valleys across the land – and instead of marking the hours it accentuated their
absence, because it always had rung ever since anyone could remember, and
it always will, marking time beyond time forever.

When I did have to leave, Suzanne and Michel would stand in the
archway and wave and watch the car out of sight. They were puzzled (not
want to go to Paris?) but pleased that I would like to live there always. They
understood with the heart – and never mind reason.

Suzanne sometimes sent us pigeons through the post. A brown paper
parcel would arrive, with the string slipping, not very well wrapped – and
once there was blood oozing out of it, to the perplexity of the concierge in
Paris who delivered the mail.

Nevertheless I used to look forward to my husband's visits, to keep the
balance. I thought the place needed him, like its core or its heart: the
overseer, the admiral of the ship (as it seemed during storms, rocking on a
high sea, wind whistling, shutters flapping; he stood looking out of the
window at the squalls, as if holding the wheel). I can see him still (though
we have both left it long since) at the time when Grospierre was alive,
sitting drinking a *canon* in the study together. They both had an equal
capacity for alcohol. My husband can mix wine and spirits in a way no one
who has seen it will ever forget, sampling direct from each bottle on a buffet
table, to the amazement of many a hostess in Paris, or an English country
house. His constitution is what the French call *une force de la nature* (and
with this he has a phenomenal endurance, a phenomenal liver, of which he
is unaware, being greatly preoccupied with cures and doctors). He has a
splendid opera voice – it could be velvet, tender, or deafening. Resounding
in the cavernous rooms of his château it was superb (and kept the ghosts in
their place) – at close quarters in Paris it was sometimes shattering. He

could be a thundercloud or witty, loving or alarming. In Paris his gramophone records were all scratched, as he did not know how to care for them – but he would play them anyway and not seem to mind. Sometimes the radio would be blaring as well, or television, or both at once, and he might decide also to play the guitar. It seemed that our universe was perpetually filled with noise, we lived in a din. In the Jura there was space, but Paris was confined. One could only admire the size of his personality. But we separated after ten years. No one before, or since, managed to live with him at all, so it can be called a success.

He was unafraid of the fiercest dogs. Once a bristling Alsatian with bared teeth sprang at us in a lonely farmyard at l'Écouvette, but he waved it away, "*Fous le camp vieux connard*, I can bark louder," he shouted, and it retreated, watching us with snarling respect from a distance. He would cross a field where there was a bull, unperturbed.

Even now, far away and so many years later, when I hear blue jays in a forest, I remember. It was the way he used to call us . . .

★   ★   ★

He sold the château. "I cannot afford to go on pouring money down a well," he said. We made over the sheep to Michel. Also there was a problem with three children (two sons from his former marriage) and the Napoleonic inheritance code; they would have to divide it and he foresaw trouble (all the more as his sons were filled with Balzacian hatred for their father and would surely behave like cruel step brothers when the time came). This could have been a tragedy – but fortunately for him he did not seem to mind, he said the château had always been such a heavy weight . . . he was nostalgic for the days, remembered from his youth, when it had run smoothly with servants, and he had never really liked our gypsy camping (so he called the summers when there was no help and I did the cooking, rushing, running – it was, however, my pleasure). He thought the place was not made for the modern world and could never be made to adapt. I thought it just needed more people to take part, a large family . . . Indeed to me the best was the rough, wild side the castle showed only when it was alone. Had the gracious waited-on people ever seen it like this?

Were they those sepia-figures in the old photograph albums, standing in groups by the front door, looking so proud? It must have most truly belonged with the men who fought with Le Flamand.

It was sold to cousins, so has stayed in the same family, and again it is through a woman that it continues. The wife's maiden name through her mother reverts to that of one of the ancestors, the lady whose portrait hangs in the sentry's hall, who hid her sons in the woods during the revolution.

This family cannot really afford it either, however. They let it for parties, for festivals, coach tours, to a psychiatrist for sessions of group therapy. There are rows of camp beds in some of the rooms, like dormitories; something has departed from the château as if its spirit is broken or its soul has flown, but perhaps only for the time being. They still call my room by my name. Most of the furniture has gone; the old mosaic floor in the hall has been taken up and replaced by brown flagstones.

Only for a traveller, seeing it from the distant hills, does it appear as it used to be, a vision in a fairy tale.

★   ★   ★

Without it our world changed, as if something inside my husband became haunted – there were spells when he lived in a lurid kaleidoscope of his own; or perhaps he had always done so, only there had not been time for these discoveries before. I preferred fear of the ghosts, whom I had grown to know and understand.

In the final outcome the castle probably does not need any one human being – just all of us like dedicated ants, fatuous perhaps, yet not so, for though we have gone our way (as others will) it still stands, through centuries of endeavour. The inside may be defaced, misunderstood or embellished by each generation of ants according to how much each one sees its point and brings out its true being – but they are all sentimental ants; and thanks to them, there it is – massive, outlasting and detached.

Through the years I often returned to the Jura – I did not leave of my own volition and for a long time part of me felt still there. One year, after skiing in Switzerland, it was near the road on the way back and I stopped to see Suzanne and Michel (whom the cousins retained), by now in their seventies and living still the same way. In winter they are alone, except for Fernand, and the château is usually empty (the cousins come to stay but do not live there). The day I visited they were waiting for a special man to come to kill their pig and prepare it. Pork has always been an important part of the winter diet in Europe. In former times of hardship it was essential, now it remains as a habit.

The killer came at the end of the afternoon, when it was growing dark. He made a huge bonfire; he slit the pig's throat and bled it. The blood is used for black pudding. Then he quartered it and put the parts into a brine barrel; the hams were hung and smoked; the perishable parts, the brain and liver would be consumed in the next days. The ears, tail and trotters are considered a delicacy.

Poor pig, king of the farmyard – he had a spectacularly gory end. The ritual was long. As night descended their figures against the orange flames looked medieval; the château loomed across the lawn, its distant silhouette clear against the night sky: my lost love, ancient, dark, and all alone.

As I drove away the angelus was sounding.

After the death of the pig I no longer wished to return, and in effect never did voluntarily, only for official purposes.

Part Two

Haute Provence

HAUTE PROVENCE

8

When my daughter was five and I was forty-six, we set off to seek our fortune. People may have difficult, even harrowing times for the sake of independence and freedom – but home is the place of the spirit, and the adventure of finding and establishing it can also be ecstatic. We moved in (by plan) and out (by fate) of several houses in England, leaving our ghosts in their gardens and a legacy of two ponds to Sussex . . . and then we came to Provence: not the well-known Alpes-Maritimes, Var or Gard, but the Haute Provence of the Drôme and the Vaucluse, which lies to the north east and reaches into the southern alps, far away from the coast, in a land apart.

The Ventoux is a moody mountain. It appears quite different according to where the traveller finds himself when he first sees it; from the road out of Malaucène to Suzette, it has a flat top like a crater and could be an old volcano; from Orange, it is simply a cone; from Buis-les-Baronnies there is a long formation of rippling stone flowing out behind like the mane of a great lion. The locals call it "Le Géant". It can be brooding under cloud, the top invisible (it is nearly 7,000 feet high) and menacing at times – at others, mellow and warm – but always it dominates. People look up at it to foretell the weather, and possibly, they say also, the future.

The valley where we lived in the Vaucluse is open, with wide views, yet is reached along small roads and has remained secret and rather private; seen from here the Ventoux sits in perfect balance, as on a throne. In autumn it is blue with purple clefts and small russet trees up its lower slopes; the top is bare rock and white pebbles. In clear weather, the sea can be seen from up there, as a brilliant line in the distance; they say the Pyrenees are also visible, the lighthouse of Marseilles and even Mont Blanc – but this is rare vision and I have never seen any of them. I did not visit the top often and never with pleasure. There is nearly always a violent wind blowing, there is something fearful about it and a person is not made welcome.

The last village in the valley is St Marguerite, small and remote, women sit sewing in doorways as they did a hundred years ago. A disused mule track winds from here to the ruined tower of old Beaumont, standing out like the roots of a tooth on the crest. The road leading the other way gradually disappears in half-abandoned lavender fields (lavender is still grown, though now it comes mainly from Turkey), but the cherry trees are cared for, their bark black against the stark white stones of the poor soil, and their old trunks are very thick.

After this the land turns into *maquis* and scrub, the track ends in a few slippery paths of scree. This side of the Ventoux is strangely quiet – rather eerie. In the woods and on the high plateaux there are boar, and a pair of eagles circles; it is the domain of wild things, seldom seen. Other sides of the mountain are civilised, with roads that have signs, and restaurants, a ski resort, an observatory – but our valley remains apart.

We arrived in Provence a decade after leaving the Jura, and lived there for three years. The plan was to stay for always but that did not come to pass; however, because it had been our intention, and because of enduring affinities, the village remains "our" village and we frequently return to it, together or with friends.

It is really only a hamlet, with two main families at daggers drawn, as is often the case in the south. They do not seem to mind. In fact they hate each other with a sort of robust enthusiasm, it is their great pleasure. They are splendid people, apart from the trait of each doing everything possible to annoy the other. But for us they would pile peaches and melons at our door, we would find tomatoes and green beans on the window sill when we came home, or beside the gate. They liked us. Perhaps, even, after the excitement of a new arrival had subsided, as the seasons passed, they saw that we loved their country and had come there to settle, not like tourists, or people with a second home. We brought all our worldly possessions, we moved in. We stayed, and lived as they lived, through the winter in the piercing cold, keeping the log fire going night and day. We had a piano and books, it was home.

The first summer, amazed by the fruit and overcome by its plenitude, I said to the old blonde lady, "Thank you but – it is too much –" and she laughed with the high metallic guffaw peculiar to her and said, "They are the unsaleable ones, otherwise we would only give them to the pig."

The pig never saw the daylight. It lived in a room like a cellar, waiting to be eaten, and probably knowing. The Faraud family all looked rather like pigs, with regular but thick features and light skins and lashes – except the dark wife who came from elsewhere (as indeed so had her in-laws, originally from the north of Italy) and could not sleep at night because her husband ran after other women. Long after she had stopped caring, the sleepless habit remained. We called the old lady "Pigga-wigger". She had faded blue eyes, very few teeth, strong bare arms that were crevassed and lined like a map, but brown and healthy like her face. The north of Italy was not really far, a few hours in a bus; she had come from there with her husband three generations ago when they were young, to pick lavender. They stayed and produced descendants and grew rich and old. Prosperity made them fat. Only the dark wife, Paulette, remained slim and muscular, her body hard.

The other family are the Paganins, whose parents are the Plantevins who live beyond the hamlet in a small, old mill. In spite of the hate, they recognize in each other, with a certain respect, the fact that they all work extremely hard. The whole Faraud family goes to the fields together, except for the young daughter who wears high heels and keeps the accounts. They grow apricots, green peppers, tomatoes, cherries, beans, melons, grapes, olives . . . The middle-aged husband drives the produce to market in his lorry, an excuse also to go away and then linger. The old Faraud man is shaky and only does menial tasks, such as taking water to the bees. There are helpers at times, Spaniards who cross the frontier in June to pick the cherries, arriving like cuckoos in season and staying two months, or as long as there is any sort of work.

Georgette Paganin, of the other family, is proud of being a true peasant, from the earth, knowing its ways, whose parents were already there before the Farauds came; they truly belong. Possibly it seems unfair to her that the Farauds are so much richer and own so much land (there are rumours about their behaviour in the war, but there is no doubt that they work hard for what they have). Georgette is an only daughter and now owns her parents' land. Her husband is an outsider, Jean-Louis, fanatic for shooting; he goes away with his dog after work is done and brings home partridges, or a hare, and he will also eat finches, robins, sparrows. He fishes for trout in the river Toulourenc and makes his own dry flies. Not long after we first arrived, he asked me, with excitement, to write to an English address he had found, for a special rod. He sold us our logs. He is a great tease and we learned to tease him back. "That old apricot tree you got rid of on us, it doesn't burn. Where is last year's wood that isn't green?" I had learned in the Jura the importance of choosing different types of wood to build the fire, some fast-burning poplar and pine to start it, then slow-burning oak or acacia to last the night, an essential factor in the bitterly cold Provençal winter. Our valley is 1,500 feet high, a three-hour drive from the sea which warms the coast. The fire in the house is like its heart. None of us except the Farauds had central heating. The Plantevins have a stove in their kitchen; Monsieur Billeul (related to the Farauds by marriage, but living outside the hamlet, down the hill below us) has a large fireplace with stone seats inside, into which creep his dogs and cats. He and his wife would sit at the kitchen table offering us, when we came, a glass of their own brew of many things apart from wine. One sort of alcohol is made from orange peel. Sometimes these drinks are good, but even if not, it would be an affront not to accept. The ritual of sitting at the table with a glass and some conversation is the custom all over France in the country regions, as I well knew. We would also visit Georgette's parents, who are still *bouilleurs de cru*, allowed by law to make their own white alcohol (*framboise, quetsch, prune*) because they always had this right as *vignerons*. It has, however, been withdrawn from their daughter, and the privilege will die with them. When the Plantevins are alone they speak together in Provençal.

The summer is as hot as the winter is cold; we would swim in the river Ouvèze and come home to eat in the cool stone kitchen, leaving the blinding light and heat outside. With lunch we drank cold red wine, which – contrary to belief – is excellent, the local wine lending itself even to being iced. (I have also had this in Estremadura and Galicia where the local wine is almost purple – there is no taste like it and it cannot be bought in shops – it is found only in cafés in its own region.) In early morning and evening we watered the terrace and left the hollyhocks and vine and fig tree leaves dripping. Tourists from northern countries have picnics; the locals go indoors and close the shutters, or sit out in the deep shade given by plane or lime trees; Jean-Louis eats copiously and has a siesta, returning to the fields only when the edge has gone out of the heat. He has very blue eyes which he creases when he looks at a person, considering them, mocking slightly, but kind, often seeming on the verge of inner laughter. He knows some English and tells whenever occasion arises how the language has 343,000 words whereas French has only 93,000. This seems to please and astonish him ("Perhaps it is 243,000," he says, "but anyway, how many!").

Georgette has chestnut brown hair and a strong face like one of the statues in the isolated church on the road near Ste Jalle. It is ancient country with types of face that seem to have always been; in the cloister at Vaison there is a Christ with horns. The square chapel at Notre Dame de Grozeau is built on the site of a pagan temple. Georgette was here before anyone, the model for the statue must have looked like her. Her eyes are very dark brown, she has a faint vertical shadow which marks each cheek, making her face even more of a sculpture, she is a beauty in an odd sort of way. She would stand looking round her kitchen and say, "What shall I give you then?" having asked casually if I would stay to dinner. Then she would move about slowly and quietly, stirring something on the stove, looking into the cellar (which is a dark room on a level with the kitchen, dug into the hill behind) – and a rabbit stew would appear, with no apparent plan, or a *purée* of aubergines with garlic and black olives, or a trout caught by Jean-Louis.

For both lunch and dinner Jean-Louis was always ravenous, and would eat a whole baguette of bread with his food. The meals were natural and easy, but important and greatly enjoyed, and there was never any flap or explanation about preparation, not even recipes: Georgette's cooking just happened, like the seasons, and according to what grew. Sometimes the most delicious oddments would turn out to have been made by her mother. If Georgette left us a basket on the doorstep it would be something special such as their first cherries, the best of what they had.

Cherries are the main crop, apart from grapes. The hillsides are covered with trees, still grown in the old way, with squat, sturdy trunks and branches pruned into parasol shapes. Further north in France the fruit is now planted in straight lines and trained along wires, but here the trees remain as they have always been, and in spring the lower slopes under the blue hills are covered in white blossom. After dinner with the Paganins there are often cherries in *eau de vie* – one or two in a little glass, to twist round and eat slowly, then sip the juice, while we would sit and talk by the fire on winter nights. They preferred the winter. There was less hard work, it was less strenuous and the days were less long. In summer Jean-Louis went to market at four in the morning, and if his tomatoes or fruit had not reached the standard for despatch outside the locality they would be refused.

Our *rapport* with the Farauds was quite different: we never ate with them, but shouted good day in answer to their squawked greetings, or had long chats by the roadside. Sometimes we had a drink with them under the big tree outside their ugly modern house which, to the fury of Jean-Louis, they had been allowed to build by the mayor. Georgette said that when she was a child they used to sit in the Faraud's old house and tell stories. But that was before television came and before the hate grew. The Paganins are annoyed that we greet the Farauds at all and would rather we scowled and snubbed them, but I refuse to do this. Why? They have done us no wrong. So then I tease Jean-Louis about his Latin habits and the need for feuds about peccadillos and the way he goes on at us because "the English do not eat bread" – not by his standards anyway. He remembers once having a meal with some English people where there was no bread at all! "But my daughter is half French," I say, "and I have lived half my life in France, and in Spain . . . We are English too, but not only so." . . . "What are you, then?" . . . "European." . . . "Well," he says, "you had an English education." So he wins.

The Paganins own much less land than the Farauds, but it is precious. Apart from the traditional crops they grow muscats and a white eating grape called *dattier*, and asparagus. The Farauds do not take Jean-Louis seriously because he was not born a peasant and was in business before he came here. They think he does not understand the land, but there he is, always out on his tractor, wearing his blue cotton cap with a visor, squinting his eyes, working the fields with Georgette and her old father who is eighty but would not conceive of stopping because he would not know what else to do. Georgette, who is still in her early forties, remembers when they had mules, and when they grew lavender. The change has come in so short a time. She knows all the paths up the mountains that are now overgrown and lost to sight for other people. She also remembers the daily routine of feeding the silkworms, and the crunching noise they made as they ate their mulberry leaves. Their frames are still in the attic of her house. A large old mulberry tree remains beside nearly every farm because silk was one of the main products. Georgette's house was formerly that of her parents, who moved out to the mill when she married, and gave up their house to the young couple, who would in their turn work the land.

★ ★ ★

Malaucène, six kilometres away, is the nearest town for shopping. It is small. It might seem that all there is to it is the *mail*, or wide main avenue under the huge, shady plane trees with their leopard trunks, where the groups of old men play *pétanque*, and the ruined castle at the top with its clock face appearing rather surrealistically out of cypress trees. (This *châteaufort* was taken by the Calvinists in 1560. Stations of the Cross are half overgrown with ivy and clematis, for it is rarely visited.) But there is an old quarter, and unlike that of nearby Vaison-la-Romaine which has been restored, it has been left to itself and is inhabited entirely by local people, ratty, poor and friendly. Our builder and our electrician both live there. No tourists wander in the streets, there is nothing to attract them; they remain in the cafés of the *mail*. The names of the streets are written in Latin – an impure Latin mixed with Provençal: *Portale Ysnardorum sive superius* (Porte Soubeyran is written below in French), *Carreira del Ulmo* (rue de la Charité in French) *Carreira Magna Sive Recta* (in French they simply put Grande Rue). Outside the archway between this quarter and the rest of the town there is a fourteenth century church built by the first Avignon pope, Clement V.

Avignon is an hour's drive away, standing in flat land that has always, from time immemorial, been market gardens. Industry has mutilated it now, there are circular roads and lorries, factories have been built on what is still the fertile plain of the Vaucluse, the Comtat Venaissin (for some of it remains) which stretches between the rivers Rhône and Durance, and up to the Ventoux. It is the Durance which irrigates the fields. The Comtat was given to the Holy See by the Crown in 1274; the papal vineyards were planted then. It was famous for early fruit and the tradition has continued ever since, for the first melons still come from Cavaillon and Orange. Supermarkets and garages now stretch along the road from Avignon all the way to Carpentras (rather lost beside this road is the small town of Monteux, still a rural community inside its old walls), but once beyond Carpentras the roads leading to Venasque and Malaucène run through unspoilt country, with vineyards, which grows increasingly hilly and is surrounded by mountain peaks of wild, irregular shape.

Though traffic eddies round the outside of Avignon's medieval walls, the town within remains as it used to be, with its large square, tall plane trees, clock tower, old streets, theatres, many churches and chapels . . . There are festivals of music and exhibitions of impressionist and modern paintings as well as museums of tapestries, furniture and medieval works. At the time of the popes Avignon was a medley of escaped prisoners, penitent brothers, bawdy inns and brothels; and Jews who were allowed sanctuary provided they paid a fee.

The pope's palace is overwhelming. It is principally two fortresses built by two popes, Benedict XII and Clement VI in the fourteenth century. No doubt a strong defence was necessary, but the palace's impenetrability seems menacing rather than protective, hardly connected with praise of God. This great edifice of pale stone, with its galleries, chapels, and audience chambers, has a system of stone troughs and channels for running water, which was remarkable domestic engineering for its time – but which did not preclude a fearful stench, of drains, especially during the summer. It was so bad that it caused Petrarch to flee to the Fontaine de Vaucluse (he had also been disgusted by the corruption, which he was to call Babylonian). He settled, and lived for many years, at the Fontaine, writing much of the *canzoniere* to the "unknown Laura" while there, and returning to it from Italy and from Avignon all through his life, as to a beloved retreat.

It is a village built round the source of the river Sorgue, which issues from a cave. In winter and spring, after heavy rains, the flow from the cave rises at a speed of 150 cubic metres a second. The sight is astonishing and alarming, so suddenly does the level reach the fig trees which grow above the cave, and so thunderous is the rush of the foaming torrent surging and racing away. It is not surprising that a monster called the Coulobre was once thought to live there – until it was exorcised in the sixth century by the bishop of Cavaillon. In summer the flow from the spring is quiet, bubbling softly into a pool – an oasis of peaceful freshness (but with too many visitors to be recommended in August).

★   ★   ★

No one ever danced on the Pont d'Avignon. It was on the island in midstream below, surrounding one of the bridge's piers, that the gaiety took place. A two-storey chapel remains, but only four arches are left of what was once a bridge with a span of twenty-two piers, built in the fifteenth century by volunteers with bishops' money, and wide enough only for a horse or for foot passengers. It took eleven years to build and was named after Benezet, a shepherd boy who was inspired to divine the place where it would be least at risk from the river currents (he was subsequently canonized). Wind and flood, were, nevertheless, too much for eighteen of its arches during the next four hundred years.

★ ★ ★

Carpentras is the large county town which was the seat of the Comtat Venaissin, until the 1789 revolution. It is walled, with horseshoe doorways. The oldest synagogue in France is here; built in the fifteenth century above a ghetto, restored and rebuilt in the eighteenth century and again in 1929 and 1958. There are candlesticks in the sanctuary and an oven for baking unleavened bread in the chamber below. In the old Catholic cathedral of St Siffrein there is a Gothic doorway, called the Jewish Door, through which converts passed to be baptised. At the palace in Avignon, a century earlier, Jews were alternately given posts as financial advisers, or banished by a sundown curfew, according to which pope was in office. The building of the synagogue a hundred years later was possibly the first sign of freedom.

There is a Comtat museum in Carpentras with coins, cattle bells and relics. Market day is Friday, with stalls in all the winding streets of the town. There is an enormous selection of the herbs for which Provence is famous; bunches of marjoram, rosemary, sage, savory and thyme, gathered from the hills. Thyme is so prolific there is no need to buy it – we used to go outside our house and pick it anywhere at all. Tarragon is cultivated, and so is basil, both the large and small leg type. (It was introduced to Europe from Africa in the sixteenth century.) Nearly every window sill in the streets of all these towns has its pot of basil. Carpentras also produces exceptional, fresh melon ice cream.

★ ★ ★

This part of Haute Provence is full of intriguing discoveries. Madame de Sévigné used to stay in the château at Grignan, the home of her daughter (married to the Comte de Grignan, Lieutenant General of Provence) to whom she wrote so many letters. She hated the *mistral* with a sort of despair. Everyone hates the *mistral*, but the local people and other residents are fatalistic and accept it as an act of God. She never grew accustomed, though passionately loving everything else about the place (she writes of "succulent doves and muscat grapes"). She died at Grignan, still only in her sixties. Later her coffin was removed from the chapel, and her head was cut from the body and sent to Paris to a phrenologist. Then . . . it disappeared. It seems incredible to think that the head of this lady could simply be lost like an old letter.

No visitor should miss a slow drive along the road from Malaucène to

Suzette, to see the most dumbfounding view of all the mountain ranges.

On the road out of Malaucène going to Bedouin, just after descending from the parasol pine forests and before entering the town, there is a small monastery of very pure beauty. The chapel is an apricot colour, surrounded by dark cypress trees, and seems to emanate happiness and peace. It can be seen from the hill before the road curves, and again from the entrance, but visitors are not allowed inside. Eleven young monks live there, their average age twenty-five. A notice on the gate by the roadside says: "Please keep silence. We are praying for you."

Saxifrage and yellow poppies grow on the lower slopes of the Ventoux, as they did at the time of Petrarch who in 1336 climbed this mountain with his younger brother. It was a long and difficult ascent on rocky tracks, leading to the summit that was still "unknown to man" at this time; they reached it scratched, and in torn clothes. In his *canzoniere* Petrarch refers to the "hard mountain" Ventosum (windy) as a symbol for reason, but the "fair stream" in the valley below is the Sorgue of his "alpine retreat". He frequently quoted Provençal poets.

Though there are roads up the Ventoux now, the top is still fiercely unfriendly, cold even in summer, with a desperate barren quality. In this land the past and the present are woven together and many things are the same as they have always been; in the twentieth century the grandfather of the mayor of our village writes in Provençal of the same flowers: *sourris a la flour que s'endor*. In the spring the roar of the waters of the Sorgue at the Fontaine de Vaucluse could make any modern child imagine a new Coulobre.

All the villages, even the small ones, are fortified, shaped by centuries of attacks by different hordes of invaders. We visited many of them on expeditions to buy wine: Rasteau, Cairanne, Seguret, Entrechaux – where there is a restaurant called the Saint Hubert, after the saint who protects hunters. The wine of the region is Côte du Ventoux, which is made from grapes of Grenache, Syrah, Carignan and Cinsault. The other local wines are of the Côte du Rhone type, the most famous being from Gigondas, a small village with grassy greensward inside its ruined castle, unlike most others where the castle is on a summit requiring a climb.

Our other nearby town, ten kilometres farther than Malaucène and more sophisticated, is Vaison-la-Romaine; there are an unusual amount of Roman remains here, and all summer music festivals are held in the arena.

The Romans built an aqueduct twenty kilometres long from the spring at Grozeau (above Malaucène on the way up the Ventoux), a few vestiges of which still remain. In the market on Tuesdays there are over a dozen different sorts of olives, honeys, and *pâtés*.

Vaison was Christian in 442, and was ravaged by Barbarians until the eleventh century; by the end of the twelfth century it had been plundered to a point where the bishop had fled. It was then that the Comtes de Toulouse built a keep for defence, on the hill across the river, on the edge of a ravine. A medieval town grew round this castle and is there today, the restored *haute ville*, its cobbled streets filled with tourists. A charming hotel, Le Beffroi, is a good centre for visiting; it has a terrace and a garden, which is rare in medieval towns where the streets are narrow and dark, the houses usually enclosed, safe inside the city walls, but gloomy. There are exceptions, of which Le Crestet, five miles away, is a remarkable example, open on one whole side with a view of the southern alps, mountains in turbulent shapes, and valleys and rivers; a view as of the gods looking down.

Our farmhouse in Hameau la tuilière © Estate of Gael Elton Mayo

9

The Farauds' invisible pig in his small stone room has lost his appetite, out of dejection probably. "Why has he stopped eating?" asks the old blonde lady, and I tell her pigs need air and light. In some countries – in England, for example, where the pork is very good – they are put out in the fields to eat cabbage stalks when the crop has been picked. "But why won't he eat?" she repeats, not understanding this electrifying information, heaving her wrinkled, strong, astonishing bare arms as she slings old melon rinds through his doorway. "Did you know," I continue, "there is a kind of pig called Tamworth with soft, silky reddish hair that runs wild in the woods? They can be bred in the open and are very good for bacon. In sunlight in the distance they could be Irish setters, they are small." By her expression I know she is beginning to think I might be mad.

The Farauds' dogs are mangy roamers, never fed, apart from bones that are flung anyhow round the house for them to find. (Inside the Farauds' house is clean, with cold marble floors, but out of doors they are squalidly untidy.) The village fountain, fed by an underground stream from the Ventoux, happens to be outside their house – so they regard it as theirs and it is strewn with their jugs and buckets and old plastic bags – to the fury of Jean-Louis and to our disgust, for it is our communal fountain. The dogs are left to forage, to bark and run wild, except for one who is always chained, to keep watch, they say. They are proud of this one, called Omar. I thought at first that he was Homard and was surprised that a dog should be called Lobster. The cats . . . poor cats – still referred to however, possessively, as *their* cats. They are also given no food, they multiply in dozens, scraggy and afraid, springing away like arrows when spoken to, except for one grey tom who was friendly, intrigued by us, and came to call often with a strange, staring face as if he was studying us. We fed him; after this the other cats would creep near but remain furtive, sitting in tree branches watching, like slightly sinister furry birds. But the tom, of evidently superior intelligence, accepted us. He knew we were all right. He allowed us our territorial rights.

The Paganins' dogs, on the contrary, are sleek cocker spaniels, brushed, combed, stroked and hopelessly spoiled, begging at table to a point where the meal can be ruined, until Georgette intervenes; for Jean-Louis is the culprit, and he especially loves the one he takes shooting. I tease him about the begging; dogs in England are taught not to do so (or were in the past) and were much happier as a result, not always expecting, settling down to their own bowl . . . but there was no way he could resist ruining his dog's liver and giving him boring manners, it was permanent snack time. This man who spoils dogs and shoots birds, rabbits and hares, also loves wildlife, he is a paradox. When the eagle occasionally flies over (it is rare to see the pair, usually one comes alone) he will rush outside and shout, "Come quickly! Look!" and point to the wing span which he guesses is three metres at least. I tell him about sheep-dog trials in England and wish he could see one.

★ ★ ★

There was a sort of silence around the building where the pig lived. We felt he had gone – though he had always been quiet, never a grunt was heard. A week later a table was set for twenty people under the lime tree outside the Farauds' house and a lunch was given to celebrate the engagement of their daughter to a Spaniard, one of the fruit pickers who would not return to Spain – they had acquired an extra hand. The pig was better off dead, he was probably eaten with lentils. His *raison d'être* had come to pass at last.

The Farauds keep their bees too near the house of the Paganins. Jean-Louis applies to the *mairie*, filing a complaint: the hives are closer than the hundred metres laid down by law. The Farauds move the bees, putting them barely one hundred metres from our gate, and then take care to cross and re-cross the Paganins' land continually, using a small path that is, according to the land register in the *mairie*, discovered to be an ancient right of way, fallen into disuse. They make sure to stay well in view and to linger. Jean-Louis rubs his hands looking gleeful and plans further irritations, at the same time swearing indignantly.

Jean-Louis is irritated by the mayor. Our district is under the jurisdiction of Beaumont, a small but important village two miles away, controlling a large area of farms. Apart from a few old houses, there is only a chapel, a co-operative for wine (8 francs a litre) and the *mairie*, a simple building with a traditional terracotta tiled floor and wide staircase. The mayor is a civilised, well-read man, director of a bank, whose grandfather wrote Provençal poetry. Once Jean-Louis ran into him when he was out shooting; the mayor was walking in the uplands and reciting verse. He greatly loves his countryside. I found this *sympathique*, but "*C'est un illuminé*," says Jean-Louis scathingly. "Nothing gets done. Building is not allowed, yet he permits the new Faraud house, he is scared of not getting their vote."

The mayor has a flat in Avignon, but his home is in the village of Beaumont up the hill behind the small church where Mass is sometimes said in Provençal. He is well-informed on politics and history. His ancestor, Carrasso, was the nephew of a cardinal in Avignon in the seventeenth century, he became governor of the community and rid the people of the malevolent Comte de Beaumont who plundered and made misery. All that remains of the count's château today is the ruin, standing out on the hill above, a pile of stones in two columns like strange horns, or a prong like a fork. The name Carrasso became Charrasse and is the mayor's name today. He told me many things, including that the Crédit Agricole is one of the four biggest banks in Europe and lends money to other banks of France. I had opened an account there in a wave of enthusiasm when we first arrived – imagining us taking our produce to market. At least we did give our 75 kilos of grapes to our builder each year, who gave us wine in exchange. He owned a vineyard and included our grapes when he took his own to the co-operative, so we had a certain amount of "our wine".

One of the Paganin's sons, Marc, took a law degree, but opted out of the world and prefers doing odd jobs. He rebuilt our wall with us, showing us how to place and fit the old stones the dry stone way, to form a terrace where the wall had fallen under the so-called olive orchard, (there are only six trees). He too is proud that his mother is a 'real peasant'. It has a quality almost of aristocracy, something a person is born with, and cannot acquire. "*C'est du bidon*," he would say disparagingly about the world he didn't want and its false values. "It's phoney like a jerry can" was his funny expression. He loved our house, which had been abandoned by a third local family twenty years before we came, when the father was killed at a crossroads on his motorbike. As a child Marc loved it as his dream house, the oldest in the village, facing south, the Reissas mountain rising at the back in goat tracks through cork oak, up to the high skyline, sheltering it from the *mistral*. He consoled us in a negative way about having to leave, by saying, "Suburbia will come. Never mind, you won't miss anything," and told us he was leaving too, he was planning to go to Peru.

On getting out of the car there is a smell of crushed fennel and thyme, the smell of the *maquis*, of the south, squashed under tyres. "*Ce n'est pas le Pérou*," as they say in French, meaning it is not the end of the world. It should not be "so far to go," so difficult to achieve, just to stay here, in other words not to have to go anywhere, or search any more. (The expression can also mean to make one's fortune, probably from Pisar who discovered Peru, and the gold he found there.) It should have been simple: a smallholding, enough land to work and live on, also to write and paint. But we had acquired the house through the old widow of the crossroads victim in a dubious sale; she withheld the fact that she owned all the land; I understood that the wilderness below the house could definitely be bought later from some other person (elderly, who had let the land go), and this seemed safe because the mayor had told me the land was agricultural and no building was allowed. I was so anxious to get the house, it was so special, and no other old houses were to be found, this one was the end of a long search. The *acte de vente* was signed in front of the *notaire* who acted for both parties, as is customary in France (where there is no survey or search) and he said nothing, although he knew. However, on our remaining patch we still had lime trees, an ancient fig that produced two crops every summer, a grape vine, olives and a small wood of cork oak behind the house. And below, the large cherry orchard run wild would surely return one day to its rightful place, part of its own domain . . . it could be of no value to any person but the owner of the adjacent house, or so we thought, and were told at the time. These seven acres led up to a strange-shaped rock called Le Saffre, weird as a huge dolmen. Ammonite fossils and teeth of iguanas have been found nearby. We were happy and peaceful at first, wandering in a tangle of brilliant yellow broom and brambles, old roses gone wild, but some still with perfect blooms, and orchids, where fifty cherry trees produced some black, some red and yellow and some dark red *reverchon* cherries of unworldly taste. It felt like our own land, and we started clearing it, until we learned it was not to be. Eventually, we discovered, it might possibly be sold for building after all, the law might be changed, and it was for this, surely, that the widow was waiting. We offered her more money than its worth, but she still refused. Then anxiety grew, and gradually became an obsession, an undercurrent that nagged. We had planned an Italian garden with jasmin and datura flowers, leading down stone steps to the field . . . would it be villas instead? And this was not the only fear. I had planned to plant a vineyard and make the land produce, it was to be part of our life . . .

★   ★   ★

Marc walks along the road with a pretty girl, carrying a bunch of wild flowers they have picked. She is "only a cousin" but it looks romantic. Jean-Louis is impatient, he wishes Marc would get on with a career like his other two sons who have safe, staid jobs in Nice, and his daughter who is reading law. But, Marc answers his father, he earns his living, he does not trouble anyone, so why not leave him alone? He doesn't want a life like his brothers, they are slaves without knowing it. He does gardening jobs, builds walls, goes off on "assignments" and sleeps in his car like a gypsy. He can wash in a stream, he doesn't care. He is free. He comes back and helps his parents pick fruit, in season. He would like to have more to do with the land, their land . . . if his father would let him. "But you could be a lawyer," says Jean-Louis, exasperated, and then Marc is annoyed and drives away in his car.

There are yellow iris around the front door in spring when the light is brilliantly strong; at night frogs can be heard croaking in the stream in the valley before it dries up with summer; there are wild narcissi in the grass along the banks. By June the leaves of the vine have grown across the trellis on the terrace, making a blue-black roof of shade. A person can sit in this cool arbour and gaze into the view and into the white heat that blazes beyond. The vine is one ancient trunk, said to be perhaps two hundred years old, planted by the front door; it is now so thick that the shutters of the window beside it will not open , completely; it is like a grape-tree. We had crops in our fashion, for it was this one plant that produced 75 kilos of grapes each September.

Jean-Louis was amazed at its capacity and marvelled that it had never been sprayed or treated like their vines, yet it had no disease. There is also a very old rose that has a twisted trunk and climbs to mingle with the vine trellis, producing still an occasional small bloom. We had lime flowers which could be sold at market for *tisane*, the best being from the Ouvèze valley which was our region, only the trees were too huge and tall for it to be possible to pick them. Apart from these, and our olives and figs, we had a vegetable garden which was a long strip of fertile land on one of the terraces. (We had taken a whole summer to clear this of six foot high brambles.)

Monsieur Billeul, when younger and more energetic, had been a prize tree-pruner. He had no time now for other people's trees, but the one beside his farm is a landmark by the curve of the road, a perfect wide horizontal shape, and he took time to prune our trees, lost in the branches on a tall ladder, one of his dogs that followed everywhere standing with his paws on the bottom rung and baying. This dog evidently did not like the idea of his master up a tree, yet could not climb the ladder – so remained in upright position and howled like a wolf to the moon. His wail lasted all the time it took for the pruning, echoing for miles. Afterwards, drinking his *pastis* in our leafy arbour, Monsieur Billeul told us about how he had been sent to Scotland in the war; he almost always spoke of this, it was the only time he had been away from home. He was entirely self-sufficient, eating his own produce; he mistrusted what was sold in shops. The baker came in a van twice a week – he accepted this and bought his bread – and he would go with his wife in their old car to Malaucène for soap or clothes, driving slowly, bumping along, waving at friends.

Billeul's instinct about food was very strong, yet he told me he had never heard any television programmes, or talks about hormones being put into meat, and irradiated food. The supermarket at Malaucène sells local goat cheese, local meat and olives, seeming more like a health-food shop than the usual store, but in spite of this, and with no apparent knowledge or reason, he would shake his head and laugh, "You don't know what you're buying!" he would say, "I just eat my own." Like the intuition of a wild animal wary of civilisation, he had an inbuilt self-defence. He ate his own vegetables and fruit as well as poultry of all kinds, and rabbits, and had his own vineyard. He also ate honey he bought from the Farauds. As well as the bees they own in our hamlet, the Farauds have hives up on the mountain-side; they harvest two sorts of honey, lavender, and *toutes fleurs*, which is from the scrub heather and whatever grows on the Ventoux. The best honey, however, comes from a village ten miles away called Faucon. True to its name, this village appears to hover like a falcon on the hill – the church bell hanging visible in an open wrought iron cage in the bell tower, and the village houses built into the ruin of the castle – especially when approached by the small road from Entrechaux. The *apiculteur*, Monsieur

Joly, also produces "royal jelly", the luxurious third type of honey that the drones feed to the queen bee.

★   ★   ★

So: an old farmhouse, a stable with huge irregular beams forming the ceiling (it became the sitting room but we always called it the horse's room – room not stable for some reason of respect for the horse's ghost). It had been a one-horse, one-pig, rabbit-hutch farm; and strange – the cellar was higher than the attic, because it led into the hill behind through a wing that was separate yet joined to the house. The attic was very long and daylight could be seen through the meridional tiles of the roof, yet when it rained it remained dry; this quality of southern houses has always mystified me. The building was in a T-shape, if seen from the height of the hill, but the front was an L-shape surrounding the terrace, open at the end forming a porch under a roof of old, faded tiles, where I planted jasmine and passion flowers. Behind there were two rooms of cool stone. One had contained rabbit hutches, the other, with a cobblestone floor, was the pigsty. Above both was a second, rather secret attic, reached by a ladder. From this little porch, where we sat, there stretched the vast, always fascinating view, containing movements, anecdotes, things happening: old Monsieur Plantevin in the field, Jean-Louis on the tractor, he would wave, Monsieur Billeul bending down over his vines, or skinning a rabbit with his wife holding it; geese and guinea fowl darting and squawking in his almond orchard, the postman stopping – a man walking up the small, white road, it was often Pigga-wigger's husband, plodding with his stick, bleary-eyed, deaf, but with a permanent rather toady smile. He trudged about the local roads every day, always very slowly. Old man Faraud was despised by his family, which was odd, he was a harmless rather simple philosopher. "*Si on ne meurt pas jeane, on vit vieux*," he would say, adjusting his hearing aid, and as if to explain his incapacities, as if the obvious fact held some inner depth.

Beyond these ant-like human activities the blue hills rise in shapes like dreams, always leading on. I have never known a view so vast and yet so amiable. In the Jura at times a person could feel overwhelmed, here it felt intimate and kind. And planing in mid-distance, our terraces descend gently onto the land below, held by lines of stone walls, made by the hands of unhurried men.

Cherry trees seen from the house © Estate of Gael Elton Mayo

10

When I found our house, (staying one summer in the region where we had previously decided we wanted to live), I first saw it one night under a full moon, going for a walk after having had dinner with a friend in a village nearby. The lime trees were blossoming in voluptuous scent – I was seized by its magic, though it was dilapidated and rotting. It was made of old stones, on its terrace a huge vine had run wild over a broken trellis. Behind it the slope of the mountain ascended in clumps of broom and cork oak to a high horizon. I had enquired of an old man standing by the village fountain (subsequently identified as old man Faraud) and learned that it might be for sale, perhaps was already sold . . . and the whereabouts of the widow – and when I met her, I agreed to buy it without even seeing inside; the site and the village were so perfect, so exactly what we had longed to find and despaired of ever finding. But when the door first opened I was smitten; it was mutilated by that other side of peasants, their fearful gentrifying bad taste. Pea-green plaster covered the grey stones of the kitchen wall (traditionally in Provence, left apparent), a squalid lavatory behind a screen in one corner – a tap and broken water heater jammed into an archway, linoleum the colour and pattern of greasy soup covered the worn terracotta tiled floor. And the fireplace . . . the chimney piece had been removed and a monstrosity of imitation brick erected, vast, elephantine, painted red with white lines on cement. The shock was appalling, it seemed to have no bearing on what the house really was. But I made plans and went to work. I telephoned my daughter at school in England, "We've got a house!" – and wrote to my two older children in America – and then, sitting outside on the simple slab of worn stone that formed a seat, I knew it was true.

Indoors, I still felt a certain alarm. With the help of a builder from the nearby town of Malaucène, we ripped it all away. We scraped and cleared and uncovered niches and strange alcoves; discovered the secret places old houses always have. Downstairs, we found a granite sink that had been hidden under junk. Upstairs was a little room with crooked walls where I learned they had hung the pig after it was killed; we turned this into a second bathroom. I found an electrician and a plumber. The last slabs of rock in the disused quarry of old Beaumont were obtained to rebuild the fireplace as it must have been, with a lintel of oak across the top in the traditional local T-shape – the stones of the kitchen wall appeared again.

At punctually a quarter to twelve each day, my rather wild-looking builder Canestrari (he had a wall-eye and volumes of excited conversation) would leave for lunch, a sacred appointment for which he was never late. He returned at about two-thirty smelling strongly of garlic and wine, and ever more talkative, waving his arms. At the end of each day he and I sat drinking *pastis* in the leafy arbour, feeling that the soul of the house had been regained, the desecration effaced, it had returned to its origins, perhaps to the days when the vine had been planted by the front door. The peace had come back. I noticed this quality all the time we lived there: a deep feeling of serenity and permanence. In the first sunlight of early morning, or when the crescent moon lay over the dark hill behind Beaumont, in the complete silence of summer afternoons at siesta time when the whole countryside might be dead – Europe seemed to hang there, ancient, timeless and forever.

★   ★   ★

The *fête* of Beaumont is in July and lasts three days. Miliotto, everyone's electrician, hangs coloured lights in the trees outside the *mairie*, a wooden platform is installed and an orchestra plays. The first year my daughter Georgia, aged fifteen, was invited to dance by the mayor's son, by the plumber and Canestrari.

There are many friends: a French painter who lives in an isolated farmhouse and exhibits in Paris; a Canadian lady who was a publisher and is now a potter, who has made a dwelling of poetic beauty in the fortified wall of St Romain; an old Russian lady who smokes a pipe, lives alone on a hilltop with a dog and three cats and never locks her door at night. She was a journalist, but retired to Provence long ago. She is very small and immensely sturdy. She restored her farmhouse herself, building stone terraces like a mason, bookcases like a carpenter, and now she keeps her house clean, is completely informed on world events, grows truffles as a crop, owns her vineyard and is over seventy. There is a French architect and his wife who came from Nigeria after independence and have made their home in the Drôme ever since . . . and an English admiral who retired to a *bastide* on a windy hill where he created an incredible garden. There is a Swiss musician (the only other foreigner in our hamlet) who plays the violin; he comes in summer to a tiny, old house with his wife and small son, has a rare knowledge of the lost mountain paths, loves the beauty of the place and goes into Malaucène to fetch the bread on his bicycle.

The Swiss musician owned a barn below his house. The Farauds asked if they could buy it and repair it for use. He did not sell, but gave it to them as a present. Instead of using it for agricultural purposes they knocked it down and built the ugly two-storey house that blocks his view on the south side. Because they are working farmers they are allowed to expand, a house has also been permitted (by the previous mayor) for their older daughter, although she is married to a *Marseillais* and only uses it for weekends; it is stucco with shiny red tiles and stands out glaringly on the hill, unrelated to local style. It is these two buildings that have brought a suburban element into the old hamlet, which consisted previously of seven houses in a line under the mountain, made of local stone and with roofs of soft multi-coloured Roman tiles.

These people and many more permanent residents have no Provençal origins, but they entirely belong and are accepted by the locals who in this region are very friendly (however a distinction is made between residents and those with holiday homes). The Russian who farms is held in special esteem; once after a disaster following a forest fire, two farmers came to call, offering to lend her money.

When we rebuilt our wall under the olive orchard we were still hoping, yet by then we knew we would almost certainly have to go. Someone who did not require land would buy the house, it would be a summer home. This made Marc angry, he hated tourists and he liked the way we had burned our bridges to be here, but he agreed that it had to be. Our last effort to buy back the land had failed. The widow was adamant and looked as crafty as usual when approached on one of our occasional visits to her in Vaison in the hideous flat where she lived, surrounded by doilies and satin cushions with black fringes, serving us her own homemade Pernod nevertheless with a false honeyed smile. This time I had offered the price of building land, far above its agricultural value, but she hung on to her refusal like the old spider that she was, with two hopeless butterflies in her web. And she always enquired about my health and said she prayed for us both when she went to Lourdes. She had loved her roses, she told us, and used to say good morning to them calling them by their names. (In effect when we cleared the *potager* I had found a Madame Meilland blooming in the rubble, brambles and old rusty cans.)

Georgette said wistfully that if only she had met us sooner, she, the peasant would have told us how to "deal with peasants". To beware of the *notaire*. The land would have had to be included in the sale. But I had bought the house before knowing Georgette. There had been no one to inform us. What land? We had not known it belonged. We were foreign suckers then, we became *Vauclusiennes* too late. It felt that the house itself had been betrayed, whoever lived in it, not just us, for it had always had its land. To sell it separately was like cutting the petticoats off a woman. When I was a child my mother used to sing me a song about an old lady who took her eggs to market and fell asleep by the roadside – and a pedlar came and cut off her voluminous skirts and took the cloth away to sell. When she woke, her clothes were high above her knees and when she got home, the dog barked and did not recognise her.

We owned the small wood behind the house, and above that it was steep grey rocks and scrub, God's country. No water, no way of bringing electricity (even if it ceased to be communal land) without passing through our property, so no one could ever build. But that was the back. What of the land in front? Marc thought there would indeed eventually be building lots; this unease ground on like a gramophone record. As the seasons returned and we belonged, it grew into a torment. I would wake in the night in alarm and wonder: should we visit the widow again? Yet to what avail? What more could she want than money? We had (trembling) asked her to name her sum. She lived too far away and was too old to work the land. Ah, but it was hers. "*C'est mon terrain*," she always said, sitting in her satin cushions, smug and safe in her ugly flat. And so I would fall sadly asleep again in the little house whose rights (with ours) had been deprived. She had cheated and won.

★   ★   ★

In July we went to the herb market in Buis-les-Baronnies; it is the biggest in France, people come to it from all over the land. The village square is triangular and surrounded by fifteenth century arcades. Buis is also a centre for olive oil, it can be tasted, like buying wine, or tea. The other centre for oil is Nyons, especially famous for its black olives. But Nyons is a happy place, sheltered, where exotic plants grow and old people are reputed to live long. Buis is different. Before going there the name is romantic and one is attracted. It is strangely situated under rather overpoweringly shaped mountains; though a beautiful little town, there is something uneasy, a veil hangs over it, indefinable, and a person does not wish to stay there long.

Marc took us to a deserted village high in the hills behind Puymeras. The road was not tarred, there were no signposts to tell where we were: it was a lost, unknown place except to him. It was where his grandfather Plantevin was born, and where he had lived as a young man. Now there was not a soul, most of the houses were in ruins, there was fennel pushing up through the grey stones of the tiny chapel and old, worn lavender like thin hair. Yet it was as serene and peaceful as Buis was hostile.

"You should buy the entire place," said Marc, "before it is discovered. But there are fifteen different owners, you would have a hard time, even for this rubble. Anyway . . . it is too late, Provence is being quietly ruined by second-home people who have suburban tastes, urban people playing at country life . . . Some speculator company will come . . . then it will be finished . . ." and he went off into his dream of Peru. The sky was a clear, intense blue, there were no clouds, only a hawk soaring and the cicadas. It seemed indeed strange that it should be too late. I wondered if he would ever get to Peru: I was anxious for him, he based his plan on a job he had been offered by a man with a record, who was waiting for his papers to be put in order to obtain a passport. And why Peru ? Because it was still wild, Marc said. Wild with revolution? With politics? But perhaps he was dreaming of huge uninhabited space, with scope for everything still to be done.

As if following these thoughts the *mistral* rose and began flattening the trees, mean, relentless. In winter it brings clear weather and chases away low clouds after storms, but is icy cold; in summer it brings madness, harsh heat like from a hair dryer. Three, six or nine days; when it comes, people start to count. We ran back to the car and drove away.

⋆   ⋆   ⋆

On the last day we walked up the river Toulourenc with Marc, wading where the river was shallow, swimming through the deep pools. At first there were naked Dutch tourists lying on the rocks, once a bearded man coming downstream with a rucksack, wearing a hat and glasses – his swinging genitals contrasting oddly with his very dressed top. After a time there were no more people, just a kingfisher and us; the river growing narrower but very blue, with clear pools, and a sort of tenderness about the conditional tense of our life vision and the friendship with Marc – could we still, by some miracle, stay? The mayor said no building would be allowed. Jean-Louis hated the mayor and did not trust him. I liked him but did not expect him to be infallible. Could we take a chance? My older daughter lives in America; I had imagined her here one day, with her two little girls, looking for crayfish in this river. My son and his wife had visited the summer we moved in, as if we were truly settling; their son Adam had helped us start clearing the brambles. It might still be . . . could be . . . a life? The house, though the sale was now agreed to a Canadian, was not yet signed away from us. (Panic. Should we not sign?) What is home? The familiar feel and smell. Belonging. Not to explain why. Where the affinities are right. It doesn't matter why. Love for a place, love.

So how could we leave it then? Yet how could we stay? The Farauds' older daughter had a right of way to cross what land remained to us with her Marseillais husband and friends in car, or walking in chattering groups, in order to reach their house in the woods beyond. (This had been granted before we came, when the house was derelict, and the widow didn't care. It was carefully not mentioned by her or the *notaire* in the sale.) They came rarely, but of a sudden, and with their arrival all privacy and rural serenity ceased. If we could retrieve our land we would give them a passage further away, out of sight and sound. If we could retrieve our land, the mayor told me the Crédit Agricole would lend us the money to plant a vineyard . . . But it was only a futile obsession . . . to retrieve the irretrievable.

Marc has very blue eyes like his father, with a southern skin, brown, diving into the water with my daughter, also brown but blonde, shrieking and giggling; Marc is stocky and strong, he can build a wall like a mason but also read and discuss his books; he likes Caine. If I had been eighteen I would have found him irresistible. Maybe my daughter did, she was eighteen when we left – he was twenty-seven. An intellectual hobo, an educated young man doing manual work.

They say the Ventoux can tell the future. When we got home it wore a rather frivolous white plume of a cloud, like a feather in a hat. It was impervious, it told nothing. There were scorpions in the house; when they come indoors the local people say it is a sign that it will rain. Dark purple grapes hung in festoons from the roof of the terrace, needing to be picked. It was September. Something was over.

Monsieur Plantevin picking figs

11

November is the miraculous month, more so than October. It is a golden colour with hazy distances and yet an ethereal luminosity. The cherry trees which covered the slopes in white blossom in spring are now scarlet, following and accentuating the shape of the land; tall poplars make vertical lines of brilliant yellow across the long, lavender hills; small swirls of blue smoke from bonfires rise here and there; and the Ventoux sits there, majestic, inevitable as the winter that is coming. The days are warm but short; the sun goes behind the mountain on our side of the Montmirail range at five exactly (I used to time it), the dark comes with no twilight and immediately brings the cold, sharp and intense. Quickly then, hurry indoors and make sure of the fire.

I spent a winter alone once, as my daughter was away at school, and I was writing a book. Although friends live within a radius of twenty miles, I did not see people in this work time. Opening the door on early autumn mornings to find the last leaves drenched; and peace. Only sometimes, dinner at night could be a bit dull. The radio, the fire, the manuscript to correct and reflecting upon this and that was usually, but not always, enough. I did not read until I went to bed. The old blonde lady often said, "A fire is company," leaning through the kitchen window with her elbows on the sill, intrigued (even astonished – she had probably never been alone in her life), and indeed it is true, a fire is a living thing. But when at times its company failed me, I played a game: I imagined a dialogue between a couple I had seen once, farther north in the Drôme, in a rather ratty village. Beyond Buis-les-Baronnies there is a high crest, then the land opens out barer, vast, beautiful, but aloof. There are tall almond trees which are very old, and lavender is still cultivated more than in the Vaucluse. The high pass seems to mark an entrance to a different world – and as if to accentuate it, there is a rather surrealist memorial stone to a young man who was "carried away by the wind". I stopped to look at it in perplexed reverence. On this day lavender was being harvested and was lying in aromatic bundles by the roadside. The two people I saw were in a small shop in the village of Ste Jalle, obviously permanent residents, and English – I found them intriguing in their old espadrilles and faded clothes, with their battered Land Rover outside. They belonged, and yet somehow they were still very much expatriates . . . there was something wistful about them that made me wonder: had it worked, leaving England and living in this remote place? Perhaps I would see them again somewhere and find out who they were – unlikely, because the land on the other side of the Col d'Ey seemed far away from us in our world of Vaison and Malaucène. Their oddness did not strike me fully until I was nearly home, and then I started the game of imagining their talk, overheard in a café, or more likely in their kitchen. After that I sometimes "went to dinner in the Drôme". It was my escape game.

Once in the middle of this, when I was writing down their conversation, like writing a play, in great spirits, the telephone rang. It was a man I had happened not to marry long ago, but with whom I had kept in touch over the years though we had little in common apart from habit and sharing the same friends. He was an extrovert and a city-dweller who could never understand solitude. (But then no more could the old Faraud lady.) "How are you getting on?" he asked kindly, or maybe hoping for an invitation. "I'm having a marvellous time!" I almost shouted – with the fire and red wine and my imaginary dinner companions I was quite excited. "What's going on, is there a party?" he asked. "No, I'm alone."

There was an astounded silence . . . this Cartesian Frenchman could not grasp that any person could be having a splendid evening all alone, merely having ideas.

Happiness is illogical, I had often tried to tell him in the past, and failed. "It can't be explained, like love it is suddenly there because of the light on the grass or some chance thing . . ." and at this moment, as we talked on the telephone there was a chance thing: the grey cat passed, saucy, slightly disturbing with his peculiar stare, pausing to look in at me. He knew about solitude. All cats know. It was as if, when he waved his tail and the next minute was gone, we shared a joke or an understanding. A ghost outlined against the last unfallen vine leaves, crossing the windowsill. A familiar. "The cat!" I shrieked, ecstatic.

"You are mad," said my friend, far away in Paris, and rang off. His life was organised, there was no chance thing.

I returned to my "dinner in the Drôme", and finished writing the couple's conversation, into which came, here and there, little snippets of their past life, painting their whole picture. But after it was finished, it was very quiet in the kitchen, the exhilaration had long died down, the telephone call had altered and interrupted the pleasure. Anyway, could the couple really be like this, or had I simply written a fantasy? Had I thought I was psychic? It didn't matter, it was only a game. I felt a little sad.

I raked the fire and separated the logs so they would burn more slowly, and then covered them with ashes to make them last the night. Then I went upstairs to bed as if I had truly been out to dinner and had just got home, having stayed too long at the party. Maybe my friend who telephoned was right. "Take your life in hand," he used to say. "Get out into the world." What world? He went to parties, he was written about in magazines . . . I had been out in that world, but it belonged now with the old dresses I still wore on rare occasions; it was more often Georgia who wore them now. Good dresses, by couturiers Rochas, de Rauch, or my own designs made by Monsieur Chevalier . . . Six cancer operations later, and a failed mad marriage, anyone would want a different world. There had been love removed by fate. There had been success, happiness, delight; but in spite of this the last years had been rather rough. I was lucky in that I was born happy. I seemed to love everything; good even came out of the cancer ward. But a person grows tired. People, their emotions and relationships and arguments, are tiring. To be alone was a sort of luxury, a physical rest. Yet was it . . . now?

There was a great orange moon over the dark crest of hill through the window, lighting the side of the Beaumont ruin with a strange phosphorescence. It was ancient, it would be there long after any of this ceased to matter. "Just let it stay the same," the man in my story had said, as I finished writing their dialogue. The couple were invented, yet they were not, they had become real to me. I would tremendously like to know more about them. I was Pirandello in search of two characters – yet not so, I had seen them in the Drôme; characters in a book grown real, yet not in a book, they existed. How could I meet them? I felt a little mad now (maybe my Paris friend was right) because I missed them, I had grown fond of them and would like to find out who they were. It was time to leave the house next week, the sale had been completed. In a way I felt I had betrayed the house by leaving it. ("No," Georgia had said, "you saved the house. It was in ruins, and before the ruins it had been made ugly. You brought back its soul.") So much for the house, then.

But what of us? Reality settled into my bedroom. The dinner in the Drôme was over. It was lonely here.

Our vine, which was supposed to be two hundred years old.
© Estate of Gael Elton Mayo

Part Three

The Jura Revisited

The church at Frontenay. Stones like milestones on each side of the path
mark the boundary of the *seigneur*'s domain © Estate of Gael Elton Mayo

12

In 1986 I returned to the Jura. Michel is eighty now, Suzanne is seventy-five; she plants and cares for the vegetable garden entirely alone. It is a remarkable acre of all manner of vegetables and herbs – baskets of which go up to the throngs of people at the château every day in summer. Apart from that, she and Michel farm for themselves. They still have twenty sheep that sleep in the stables and are put out to pasture by day in various orchards and fields. Fernand is still there, twenty years on, with his badger-bridegroom smile showing his gold tooth, making the same cheeky suggestive jokes "Are you going to swim in the river? Will you soap my back if I come too?"), his belly ever-bigger between him and the table. He still hauls huge logs with his tractor. Randez and Tourez have long gone, there are no more wild men living in the woods, nor is there a resident priest. The priest's house has been bought by the de Rougement family and beautifully restored. The room with the slender column and vaulted ceiling (where the sow gave birth to eleven piglets) is now their kitchen. The Mass for three villages is said by one priest who lives in Passenans. Milk is fetched from the farms in huge trucks and taken direct to factories, the cheese-making "chalet" has gone, the cheese is less good (except that from Poligny).

One day recently a *gendarme* who happened to call noticed that the pool below the spring at the grotto had silted and grown shallow. Michel told him he had given up breeding trout because he was too old to keep up the clearing and dredging. The next day, six young *gendarmes* from Domblans appeared and in one afternoon they cleared the pool. Suzanne delightedly gave them wine, bread and sausage, *"Nous avons trinqué"* – "We drank on it together" – she said, and as a result there are now trout again. Their water is cold, pure and fast-running; Michel only half-feeds them, so they eat flies and their natural food, and are as delicious as when long ago trout was considered a luxury.

My husband still owns a small house below the vegetable garden, built into the high wall. It opens onto the church lane: a queer, poetic and very old house, where Apollon died – the deaf-mute whose foot was eaten by a rat. It has been restored and repaired in rather chaotic fashion, and is furnished with pieces from the château, the ancestors' portraits looking slightly vexed. The rusty weather cock with German bullet holes is over the door, a cherished relic. A room with a vaulted stone ceiling has been converted into a dining room with some rather incongruous English Regency chairs and table – all covered with mildew as the room was originally a cellar and is very damp. The room next door is a muddled kitchen with a tapestry hung like a curtain across the middle. Upstairs there are bedrooms opening onto a wide terrace with the great and famous western view, seen now closer at hand in a more human focus. The wild (somewhat disturbing) southern view does not show from here. There is an outside staircase leading to rooms at the top that open onto the vegetable garden.

The former *châtelain* does not like the Jura, so the house is for sale. His dislike is not for the reason one might suppose – because his little house is under the lee of his lost château. About that he has no regrets, saying frequently that he is glad to have its heavy weight off his back (unlike his daughter and myself), and his only complaint is that it has been made ugly. But to him the Jura is lost. Many new buildings outside the villages are cement and do not fit into a rural scene; the smallholders wear mass-produced clothes and have lost their character. "They used to have horses," he says. "It was elementary, the dung was put on the garden,[8] it was not called 'organic cultivation'. Sabots were made of local wood." A feudal point of view perhaps, but also an artistic one. "And," he adds, "the September pilgrimage to the grotto has become a disaster." In his youth farmers came with donkeys, visitors came with faith. Now there are hundreds of cars and long after the Mass is over blaring radios fill the air and the ground is covered with picnic litter. By nightfall, though, only the faithful remain. They walk chanting, in torchlight procession, up the path from the church through the château courtyard (the priest having asked permission, which is always granted), and return to the grotto to bid the Virgin goodnight.

---

[8] Suzanne still uses no fertilizer but dung on her garden, including that of their horse, who died age thirty, six months ago, and whose manure is carefully saved for next winter.

Building is an important subject. The new ones look wrong not merely because they are modern but because they are designed without regard for their surroundings. In former times houses belonged: local materials, weather and agriculture dictated their appearance. In Bresse corn for the famous chickens (*poulets de Bresse*) was hung to dry under the eaves, so the long one-storey houses of pink brick had wide over-hanging roofs making porches supported by slender columns. Higher up, where it was cattle country, the thick-walled stone houses had wide arched doorways at one end for the cows, house and cattle stable being contained in the same building. In Auvergne, which has very wet winters, the roofs are steep and are made of locally quarried slate so that the rain can slide off easily. In the south where it is hot, the roofs are almost flat and are made of Roman tiles – terracotta is made locally – with spaces to admit air. So apart from being functional and practical, each region's houses had their own distinct character and had been built without hurry, following the traditional designs of the master masons, the *genoises* or beading under the eaves applied with pleasure. For there was time . . . Cathedrals were built by men who never saw or expected to see the finished result, and in a smaller way that spirit of pride in craftmanship had been general.

The *enlaidissement,* or uglification, seems to be particularly sad in the Jura. In most regions they try to conform to the local style, but in the Jura they default, and a jarring mixture results. "One might as well be in Clamart, or any ugly suburb of Paris," the *châtelain* says. "The same breezeblocks all through the land." At one time he was in charge of building permits for the whole of France, and tried hard to make each region see the point of its heritage. The ugliness to be seen now is aggressive. Domblans and Voiteur are nearly joined up, the two kilometres of road between them have a large scattering of houses which are the work of the local builder, Boudier, who encourages the new anything-goes-style which has made his fortune. Tethered in the orchard of a twelfth century farm which sells goat cheese, the billy goat looks stranded.

Nevertheless the Jura retains its beauty. Near conglomerations it may seem like a tamed creature to those who knew it before, but on the high land at l'Écouvette and the Roman road from Plasnes to Château Chalon it continues to be its true self – a country of quiet hidden lakes, tall forests, pied-orange salamanders and lilies. In May and June there are carpets of wild flowers in the meadows that are long lost elsewhere: tiny pansies, crimson clover, lovage, viper's bugloss, harebells, mignonette, columbines, carnations, cowslips, spotted fritillaries. In September autumn crocuses spread a lavender haze over the hills. Infinity is contained in the vastness of the long views.

The cyclamen that were protected round the grotto of Varroz used to grow also at Frontenay in the avenue of old hornbeam trees (they were specially loved by my husband's father). In florist shops in towns this flower, sold in pots, is floppy and hard to care for, wilts easily and is often sickly. But when wild it has a delicious pervasive scent and is hardy; it comes up year after year, tiny as violets – and has been doing so for three hundred years, since Lacuzon. At Frontenay now though, they have been trampled by the crowds.

13

The approach to the Château de Frontenay is not a formal drive, but an avenue of trees which might simply be a woodland lane. The first part is in the open, with meadows and cows grazing, then it enters deep shade and along the roadside in spring there is wild garlic in a mass of white flowers like stars. On the left, behind piles of large logs, the hill rises into the forest; a steep path (now a narrow tarred road) descends to the grotto; under the tree branches on the right stretches a blue haze – it is odd to be enclosed in trees and yet perceive such an immense view. Everything is odd, there is an underlying strangeness about it all.

The gatehouse is set at an angle so the château cannot be seen until a person is inside the archway. Then . . . there it is across the lawn. This position of the gate, which probably happened by chance when it was built over the fortified ditch, means that the castle is suddenly and unexpectedly close and the visitor is seized. Before arriving it has been far away, seen across the surrounding land – and according to the viewpoint has appeared to be on a cliff, or in rolling fields, or, from the high road, part of the hill crest. But always it has been distant, a mirage perhaps.

Alas, inside the gate, now, the true enchantment has gone. No more jackdaws circle round the back, they have even left the churchyard. The ghosts must have fled too, there are so many people about in summer, groups of forty-strong straggle about the lawn – it seems like a public park. My husband is angry at the uglification inside, but it is perhaps inevitable if it has to be let. The cousins are welcoming, kind and unaware.

★ ★ ★

In the churchyard there is a tombstone with an inscription that is a quotation from the last line of a poem of Baudelaire: *la servante au grand coeur*. It is the grave of my husband's nanny, to whom he was devoted. His mother died when he was eight, he had a love-hate relationship with his older sister who was bossy, and it was the *nounou* who brought him up. She was a very small peasant lady who came to the family when she was over sixty; she warmed his underclothes by the fire, spoiled him and taught him no manners. When she died in Paris he drove her coffin to the Jura on a trailer behind his car – though this is illegal – and buried her with deep sorrow.

His parents lie in the family vault which is in a small chapel at the end of the avenue of lime trees beyond the church; this land formerly all belonged to the château, but has been given to the *commune*, except for the chapel which he did not sell with the castle. There are two large stones with swords engraved on them that head the avenue at the church steps; these marked the domain of the *seigneur* and his rights.

An early ancestor, the Comte de Visemal, is inside the church and has a slab on the floor – there are pews on top of him now because it is so long since the family attended Mass that care is not taken. (He was the last *châtelain* before the conquest and perhaps deserves better.) The church is of twelfth-century origin, set below the château on a wooded rocky shoulder. A tunnel leading from the chancel into the cellar of the château has now been blocked.

There is room for one more in the chapel; when his time comes, my husband may be laid to rest there and will close the chapter of his own line at Frontenay, which is in itself the last of the *vieille garde*. He has always held that though the day of feudalism has passed, a title still carries obligations and is not just an empty form of introduction used at white-glove dinner parties.

Apart from bringing electricity and water to Frontenay, and giving endless help to the people and job guidance for the young, he also started the first government housing plan in France with "moderate rents" after the war, when there was a dire shortage. Later he regretted the aesthetic result, when I.L.M.'s[9] sprang up in the form of urban blocks of flats outside old villages and towns – but the human need had been too urgent to spend time on architectural research.

He views Paris, where he lives, in rather the same light as the modern development of the Jura – "full of vulgarians now". In this aspect he bears a resemblance to the Baron de Charlus (based on Robert de Montesquiou)

---

[9] *Immeuble à Loyer Modéré*

in Proust, who had many titles, some of them princely, and who already in the nineteenth century found the world was "going off", and used to say, "If one wants to travel incognito nowadays the best thing is to use the title of prince, there are so many about it is very common and passes unnoticed."

He steps out of the front door into his street, looks about disparagingly, like Charlus, often wearing a black hat and a cloak – a slightly alarming figure, then he clears his throat with an ear-splitting noise like a whip-crack, and spits. So much for what the world has become.

When he reached retirement age he was enjoying his job as Inspecteur Général de l'Équipement in the Ministere de l'Aménagement du Territoire, de l'Equipement, du lodgement et du Tourisme (the Ministry of Public Works and Construction) and did not want to leave, so . . . he simply stayed on. By managing to become an *agent contractuel,* in he went each day with his faithful secretary (also officially retired); an old maid with a quality of devotion akin to that of a nun, or a saint (or perhaps simply she loved him, in her platonic and respectful fashion, for she is still there and has been with him for over forty years through all his appointments). They would sit down and write letters on government paper, airing ideas, and taking useful charge of many problems, holding a twilit power over various projects, saving beauty, protecting sites. This lasted many years, until a young socialist chief of staff was appointed and told him firmly to leave, to his great annoyance.

Recently he was invited by the Fondation du Futur to an anti-terrorist meeting. He observed that they did nothing but tell anecdotes about what everyone had already read in the newspaper; he stood up to say so with some vehemence and was not appreciated. So he is now drawing up his own campaign plan, dictating the manifesto to devoted and unpaid Mademoiselle R. She also accompanies him on trips to the Jura with his car full of all the unwanted furniture and trappings and never-to-be-thrown-away objects that get in the way in Paris, which they unload into the repository of Apollon's small house – where it will mildew through the damp, freezing winters, gradually subsiding into piles of broken antique legs and dormice turds for years to come.

One day a buyer will appear, an artist probably, or a poet, who will be beguiled by the queer little house – and perhaps in the pile of oddments s/he will still find a treasure.

★   ★   ★

Before leaving the Jura, my daughter and I walked in the forest, searching for old landmarks. There is no trace left of le Fritz's house, yet part of him – and of us – will always remain in those woods. I made three other visits: the grotto at Baume-les-Messieurs is browner than in the lyrical description by Jouhan, the lakes are shallow and there are no longer so many bats, but it is still a phenomenon, seemingly so many miles of labyrinths and tunnels. The height of the ceilings is giddy-making, visitors crane their necks, looking up into concentric circles with walls of thick fossilised mud, like elephant's hide. The guide has taken to playing a horn, and a recording of Wagner; it is deafening and terrifying, one is enclosed claustrophobically in a vast crescendo – what if it should go dark, if the electric lighting should fail? Could the vibration not blow a fuse? Then the visitors would trample each other and panic . . . It would be so easy to get lost in these wet black passages leading to the insides of the earth.

Syam: the yellow Italianate villa with green shutters (which was inherited by Sadi Carnot from his second wife) is now lived in by his daughter, Fernique Nadaud des Islets, and is open to the public two days a week. It still has the private quality of a house in a novel. The boat-shaped sofas, statues in alcoves, all the furnishings, curtains, even the door handles are in the style of Napoleon III, yet it is small and warm. The house sits in a wide valley surrounded by wooded mountains shaped like dreams, often shreds of white mists float horizontally across them – it seems cut off and beyond the tangible world, as if Sadi, "the musician who talked to roses" left some of his strangeness behind.

The final and most memorable visit was to Georges Rabuz, the farmer whose steep vineyard was just below the château. He used to work it with two black mules and it was on to his land that the walls rolled down, the day of the avalanche. From him we used to buy yellow wine, sitting in his kitchen, feeling the 14 degrees bring wildness into his talk. Suzanne told me he had been ill.

His house is in the lower part of Frontenay called Vaux, in a crescent of buildings with wide doorways for the cattle. He explained that he had had *la maladie des rois* (he pronounced it *rey*) as they called it locally; it consists of an unquenchable nosebleed, comes to his family in their old age and had just killed his sister. It would seem to be a sort of haemophilia – incredibly – for it is three hundred years since the Spaniards left. Perhaps what has been handed down is a collective memory. Yet it is a physical reality (could it be from inbreeding?) and is apparently called "Rendu Osler", diagnosed by an American and treated in the hospital in Lyon, where he had been taken. They asked if he would be prepared to be a guinea pig for their new cure, and he readily agreed. "I am seventy-six," he said.

The cure must be working, for he seems miraculously recovered, though he must take many pills which he says make him forgetful – yet his conversation was brilliant, if rapid and sometimes disjointed. He told all kinds of local tales. The neighbour had burned all his identity papers in the oven of his stove because he was so fed up with government interference. "There are no more peasants," he said, with the same pride in his lineage as Georgette in Provence, and the same regret. "There used to be thirty-two of us with vineyards, now there are only three – Jobez, Bailly and Guichard. Guichard also has a hundred cows and works with his three sons. [10] But my children have all gone to the towns – why? Because the Crédit Agricole and the S.A.F.E.R. [11] interfere in everything, the young are hemmed in by rules and don't like it. I have sold my land – half to your cousin at the château and half to S.A.F.E.R. I tried sheep first but it did not work out – only Michel knows about sheep. Your cousin has left the land fallow and doesn't use it."

Then – the only time he paused for breath – he gazed dreamily out of the door in a cloud of nostalgia, and made a quiet, extraordinary statement, "We had liberty once . . ." *We had liberty once.* "So what of the progress that is supposed to have made people free?" I asked. Then he started again, returning to the present and speaking fast: Only regression. Nothing is the same. His parents and grandparents drank masses of *gnole* every night (they were still allowed to be *bouilleurs de cru*) yet all of them lived to be eighty-five and never wore glasses, or lost their teeth. Now hay is rolled into huge bales, it remains damp inside and ferments, so when the cows eat it they get drunk and sleepy. Meat is tough. Those chickens that used to run about through the village had real taste. He even spoke of acid rain. I wondered if

[10] A reversal of former times when ten cows was the usual number. In those days many farmers owned a few cows each; now many cows are owned by only one farmer.

[11] Société d'Aide Financier et Rurale. This organisation is supposedly to give help, but farmers are always suspicious and have little good to tell of it. They think it is big business disguised.

this might be the reason Suzanne's green beans are not quite the same as before, in spite of no chemical fertilizers . . .

He wished there were neighbours, he said. The man who had burned his identity and family papers had died. Before that he had stopped eating, stale pots of food lay about, there were rats running up the walls, he got cats for their riddance and put ladders for the cats to climb . . . (the last eccentric *Jurassien* perhaps). After being ill and selling his land, Rabuz said, it was lonely, just sitting here, "But the old are dead and the young have gone." The houses beside his stood empty, their roses and hollyhocks unkempt. No more cattle or black mules ambled through the wide arches.

He waved and waved as our car left, watching us out of sight the way he might watch the back of a train, the familiar world receding. It had been his château too, his people up there, the new ones didn't know him, they didn't come to call. He had last seen my daughter when she was a small girl. She had returned to visit him now tall and twenty-two.

The next day, when we left, there stood Michel on the terrace calling to his sheep, "*hé là-bas, ohé la,*" as they clambered down with their bells jangling to graze under the fruit trees surrounding the *potager*. The angelus was tolling, Suzanne, with the usual bandana round her head was bending over her vegetables in the early morning before the heat . . . and it did seem to retain a pastoral permanence.

Part Four

Provence Revisited

The view from our sitting room © Estate of Gael Elton Mayo

14

It is 1,000 kilometres from Calais to the village where we once lived in the Vaucluse. There is time on the road to give much thought to what one may find again, and have many imagined conversations with the people there. After leaving the motorway at Bollène the road becomes small and crosses miles of vineyards in a flat plain. Then the first humpy dromedary hills appear, and already the Ventoux can be seen beyond, with the jagged line of the Dentelles de Montmirail to the south – and in spite of the excitement, and the odd impression of going home, there comes also a feeling of apprehension . . . How much will it have changed, how much more may have been lost? It is not the length of time we spent there, but the intention we had to stay forever, that made a feeling of belonging.

The old Faraud man has died. His family (wife, son, daughter-in-law and their daughter) had all gone off, gaudily dressed, on a package tour to the Canary Islands, without taking him. They found him unacceptable with his bleary smile, watery eyes and maladjusted hearing-aid, and always treated him as a useless old fool. So – he also went off, on foot down the road to Malaucène, accepting a lift, then by bus to his old village in Italy near the frontier at Briançon. He sat there in the café for a week, talking heavenly platitudes with those of his old friends who were still alive. Then he got into the bus, came home again, and after he got back, he got into his bed and died.

The grand-daughter who married the Spaniard has had a baby. Jean-Louis tells with great glee, rubbing his hands in pleasure, that it is hideous and looks just like the old man. So far, nothing has changed very much . . .

I had thought rather specially of Jean-Louis through the winter in London, each time I bought a *baguette* from the French baker in Brompton Road. There is something endearing about the way his rather harsh, teasing outside is betrayed by the shrewd-yet-tender look from his blue eyes, summing up, wondering. Now here he was, a little changed after all perhaps, once we were sitting under the trellis and I observed him more carefully. He was tired. He felt older, though he did not look it. He had dreadful backache and disc trouble – but this did not prevent him from being more of a huntsman than ever, Georgette said, going off all day in the season with his favourite dog, Piccolo; needing to be in the open, yet a fanatic for preserving wildlife, admiring enthusiastically the creatures he had such an urge to kill. The second dog, called Noyon, is left behind. This dog does not like shooting, will not retrieve, (perhaps a superior fellow, though viewed with scorn). There is a new third dog, Valli, silky and golden, a true shooting dog; the others are both Cockers, Piccolo is yellow, Noyon is black. They all have improved table manners, on this Georgette has won – except for one dreadful moment when the favourite, suddenly, with two paws on the table swiped a whole baguette of bread. Then a small whip appeared, a type of cat-of-nine-tails, and a very soft beating was adminis- tered, more like a caress. There is a third cat, born in the barn, but tamed, who leaps onto the stove and tucks in. This new cat sits on Georgette's shoulder like an owl all through dinner. He loves bread; if she hands him up a piece he will spring away and devour it in a corner, then return to her shoulder again, not demanding – and will just sit still, purring, but he will shy away if approached by any other person.

Jean-Louis is indignant and very angry that someone has shot one of the eagles. This he cannot conceive – they are quite outside his hunting, and anyway not "game". He indicated, at our first lunch, that he suspected who was guilty, and that if it were so, he would see that they were punished. He did not say the name without being sure, which was correct according to his scruples, but any harm to the eagle was a crime. "Superb!" he used always to shout, running to fetch us to admire when one or the pair would fly over. (The conditional tense again, those winter evenings of talk by the fire, when later he would escort me home with his lantern, "home" in our hamlet.) Eagles mate for life, so now one would be alone.

Many things had happened to Marc. He did not go to Peru. The man in charge of the expedition did not succeed in obtaining his own passport – probably because of his record . . . it appeared also that it had not been Peru that was intended, but Paraguay. Marc is not deterred by being laughed at. He believes in dreams. Also – he fell in love. His family did not understand. "She is fat," they said, "and without wit, not even French, a German girl called Claudia." He showed me her photograph. Her face has an intriguing elfin expression. He lived with her for a year-and-a-half in Dijon where she had a job, and he was working for a diploma in viticulture, which he obtained – the *Brevet de Technicien Supérieur en Oenologie*. After this he was offered a job in America by a wine company. Jean-Louis' pleasure was enormous, understandably – a peasant from Provence off to the U.S.A. But Marc refused the offer because of Claudia. It was his first real love, before that he had merely had girls and been a heartbreaker.

Three weeks after he refused the job, Claudia left him. (I had, received a wild letter about this in England, without many details.) This could have broken his faith in humanity as well as his heart – and for a time, it seems, it did so. But he was offered another job – and the immense drive of this young man, the quality that makes him apart, has made him now, a year later, chief in charge of a large vineyard in the Corbières. He has seven labourers under his orders, two secretaries, his own flat. It is a worldly success. At first Jean-Louis was delighted – his wayward son, so unlike his two brothers had finally settled . . . But had he?

He does not like the countryside of the Corbières. And he has another dream: he has found a half-ruined hamlet for sale on a hilltop near the Lubéron, where, if he could only buy it, he would be his own boss, for it is surrounded by a hundred acres of its own land, part of which is a forty acre vineyard. The wine is *appellation contrôlée* Côte du Ventoux. And it is beautiful . . . red earth . . . real country . . . a view of the Ventoux to the north, of the long, Lubéron mountain to the south . . . He learned of it through another *viticulteur*.

Consternation consumes Jean-Louis. This son who, a few years ago, would sleep in his car and wash in streams, was now on the way to becoming a complete success. Could he not let things develop . . . could it not last? Why can't he settle? And how could he buy this new dream anyway, what with? And why is it for sale? He is thirty – what will happen to him if he goes on like this?

★   ★   ★

The mayor has allowed only a few houses to be built since we went away. He continues to try to accomplish his aim of keeping buildings immediately beside villages or farms, not scattered over the hills like a growth of toadstools, for in other areas round Vaison or Carpentras this is what has happened. In the old view there was a wide landscape with villages in clusters – now there is a gradual covering of the land with little dots, houses that conform to the rules of local style, but are made of shoddy material and with industrial tile roofs; dwellings that look like wafer biscuits. Roman tiles, as they are called, are soft, differently graded colours; the factory ones are harsh crude red, or all flat yellow.

In a different way from Marc, the mayor is also a dreamer. His house is filled with books on the history of Beaumont (one written by his grandfather), about the time when it was called Beaumont d'Orange and "owed only to God". It was a free zone without taxation, the king had no right to their possessions. The master was the local *seigneur*. The mayor's ancestor, Antonio Carrassa, was the first outsider to be chosen when in 1630 a good governor was needed.[12]

Monsieur Charrasse today is also a good mayor in the modern sense. He has allowed the building of a ski resort on the other side of the Ventoux, which brings money to the community – but no building beyond necessity for farmers or their workers' families is allowed in the valleys of Beaumont and Ste Marguerite, which are among the last that still remain the way the northern Vaucluse has always been. Mayors of other neighbourhoods nearby have not managed the same; perhaps they do not care, or the difficulties to overcome are too great. Here, this region remains apart. At the end of the last valley, beyond Les Alazards – where the road turns to a track and runs out, leading to a forest – a friend who was exploring there was unexpectedly surrounded by a group of wild boar, and not too reassured, climbed a tree to wait until they dispersed.

Here, then, is where Jean-Louis can live the life that has always been, partly thanks to the mayor he so dislikes. He drives a tractor instead of mules, but he has kept what he calls his wide sky. He is furious about two new houses in the village, though they do not show in his view. He says the mayor allowed them for political reasons. The mayor says the Farauds (large landowners now) had to have room for their family and their workers; the mayor succeeds in making the present a continuation of the past, not a disruption.

[12] Antonio Carrassa: nephew of Cardinal Philippe de Carrassa under Pope Clement VI, married into the community of Beaumont. It was his "intelligence, culture and gift for organisation" that caused him to be chosen by the dying Maître to succeed him. (*Archives, Villeneuve-les-Avignon*).

A Mass is held, as it always was each September, at the tiny, isolated chapel of St Roch, to bless the vines that stretch around it; prayers for rain are sent to St Sidonie in spring. In former times a pilgrimage to this saint went up the side of the Ventoux asking for a blessing for the crops. Skulls with big molars have recently been found again in the Reissas mountain, behind our hamlet, memories of an ancient time that seem to lead smoothly into ours.

I see our house in the distance, with its face looking out across the valley, the oldest in the village. The Canadian who bought it is pleased, and that is enough. To return to our village and see friends is part of the continuation, but to enter the house would be going back.

No villas have been built on the land below, as Marc feared – so long as the present mayor remains it seems safe. The land has been let to a smallholder in Beaumont, who has cleared it and cut the cherry trees down. The tangle has gone, taking some magic away, but the stone terraces show clearly – it is tidier now.

★ ★ ★

Buis-les-Baronnies is ruined by crowds, cars and rattiness. Change and growth formerly meant evolution, not a crush of outsiders who do not belong. The first tourists were interested observers, not a litter-spreading mob. But once over the crest of the high pass above Buis, you look down onto the hinterland of the Drôme and see it is unchanged. There are hardly any buildings. Its immensity contains something pure – a person can feel like Cortez, coming up over the summit and leaving the world of Buis behind – a new horizon to gaze down upon: stretches of tawny hillside, dark vertical cypress, old gnarled almond trees rarely seen elsewhere so tall, brilliant lavender. On the crest, which is the Col d'Ey, there is that strange memorial stone to a young man who disappeared which I always found haunting, for it is not explained.

In Ste Jalle I wondered if I might find my couple again, with whom, on the last night in our house I had had an imaginary dinner that was oddly so real it was often in my thoughts. They were nowhere to be seen. Of course not, why should they be? It had only been a flash view, three years ago. Just that they had seemed like residents . . . I hesitated but finally did not ask the patron of the café where I had lunch, whether a rather threadbare English couple, whose name I did not know, lived nearby . . .

There were only local people in the café where I sat out on a small terrace above a river. Ste Jalle is a quite ordinary village with a castle – and a mile outside, alone by the road, a little church with a rich, intricately carved Romanesque doorway. The guide book does not mention this church, yet it is astonishing. Inside it is bare, clean local stone, in simple proportions. A baptism was taking place on the day I went there. I only met one car on the road back and over the pass again down into the crowds of Buis.

★   ★   ★

Malaucène is wonderfully unchanged; the same groups of old men playing *pétanque* under the plane trees in the *mail*, the same jumble of summer tourists who were always there, in the last few years anyway, and are pleasant. The same familiar faces to run into, the man from the *cave coopérative* who was kind enough (three years later) to say, "We haven't seen you lately, how are you?"

The old notary who rooked us has retired. The new one is a dashing, dark man, young and stout, he obviously eats well, perhaps as a result of his clever plans for buying up old houses. He appreciates foreigners who restore them better than the local people. He is open-minded – not introverted and suspicious like the Balzacian Maître Dreuilhe. With the new Maître Dejean we might have fared better concerning our house.

★   ★   ★

All the fruit trees are sprayed now; when we left, there were still some farmers who did not do this, their stands in the market had "natural produce". The trees below our house had no treatment, and their fruit tasted entirely delicious, unlike any cherries I have ever eaten or ever will again, but possibly this was a fluke and would not have lasted. I am not convinced though, since they had been abandoned for twenty years. But Madame Plantevin maintains that trees not sprayed would be infected from the other surrounding orchards, even miles away, the disease carried on the wind.

Marc is very fond of his grandfather and associates him with his hoped-for *domaine*; comparing it with his grandfather's ruined birthplace where he took us, called Les Géants (from Jayants). This is the last place in Provence where a wolf was seen, it is in their family records. In 1896 the great grandfather Plantevin was peeing by the roadside when a wolf jumped clear over his head and disappeared into the scrub on the bank.

Does the old man know of Marc's plan? All his family might well have their opinion confused by the tiring quality of their lives. Jean-Louis and Georgette do not ski any more, though the Ventoux is near and they are both excellent skiers (she was once an instructor). Their entire living comes from fifteen acres of land, with no help except from the old man, who is beginning to flag. They planted six hundred new mixed fruit trees last spring. (Cherries and plums sell at 15 francs a kilo, but they will not produce for two years.) There is a virus that will suddenly single out and strike one cherry tree in an orchard, usually a sturdy and healthy one, and it is as if it has been burnt. The leaves turn brown, it shrivels and looks scorched. The cause has not been found. Since it is unknown, it could become a plague . . . Happenings of this sort create little enthusiasm for new projects. When Jean-Louis goes shooting he maintains he is bringing home the food, which indeed he does: partridge, hare, woodcock – also trout fished from the Toulourenc – but it is probably also a form of escape from the land that is so very demanding. Perhaps this is why he is anxious about his son. Does Marc know how hard life will be when he is older, and does he know how soon he will be older? It may indeed be just the reason Marc wants a hundred acres instead of his parent's fifteen – because he knows.

★   ★   ★

Truffles have gone up in price to about £200 a kilo. Their reputation for luxury may not be understood by those who have only eaten them in restaurants, or as a barely perceptible slice in *foie gras*. Before they were grown as a crop, the smallholders, occasionally finding this treasure in the woods, would roast them in the embers and ashes of their log fires; the taste they have cooked this way is the origin of their fame. Our old Russian friend, who farms them, slices them in beaten eggs and lets them lie for three days before making an omelette. She planted the small type of oak tree (under which truffles grow) fifteen years ago and waited five years before she infected them with the germ that makes the fungus, then another five years for them to produce. They now bring her about £3,000 each autumn, sent to Hédiard in Paris, and form an important part of her living. The peasants eat them no longer, unless a wild one is occasionally found.

It would be interesting to know who was the first man to whom the peculiar idea occurred of tasting the rather horrid looking toadstool that was rooted up by a boar . . .

The last flock of sheep have gone. We used to see them on the hills, with a shepherd and a dog, and the man always waved. In former times sheep were a part of local living. Now, it is felt they are more trouble than they are worth. The habit of minding them, spending the day straying after them across hills has been lost.

It is a myth that the climate in Provence is ideal. Intense cold frequently kills the olive trees in a bad winter; in the summer of my return the heat wave was so unusually fierce that Jean-Louis said, in astonished indignation, "The heat came inside the houses this year," as if it were an affront. It had never happened before that the thick stone walls had lost their coolness; they had always been a sure refuge. And there is the demoniac, wracking *mistral* . . . It is in no way soft like the Tarn-et-Garonne and other gentle regions of France, but it has always drawn people with a voluptuous plenitude of fruit and flowers, land that smells like a wild garden, aromatic herbs . . . perhaps it casts a spell. Provence is where the troubadours sang.

Marc rebuilding our wall © Estate of Gael Elton Mayo

15

Dreamers can be dangerous. In the winter in London I had received a letter from Marc, enclosing photographs of a very small group of houses in a russet haze with blue mountains behind them. His letter was lyrical, "The earth is a rose colour, or like garnets perhaps. The houses are of old ashlar stones, there are cherry trees, a lime tree, a pine wood, large vineyards (one's own wine) – the press and bottling equipment are complete in the wine vault." This was the Domaine des Coquillades, near Gordes.

The Crédit Agricole was prepared to lend him 350,000 francs and he might raise more. It was for sale only to an *agriculteur* for the land, but he could make a company out of it, with shares, and the houses would belong to the shareholders. He had heard about it privately, it was not on the market. Probably £100,000 altogether would be needed. If I came in as partner we could restore the houses and let two of them – we could each keep our own living quarters – this, and the sale of produce and wine could make it commercial. There were two good houses and two others in ruins . . . It was like his grandfather's village, it was what we had both wanted . . . did I remember? Indeed I had never forgotten.

We arranged to meet in Paris, where he would be on his way to Lille for his present job, taking orders for Corbiéres (still safe, the manager of a company). How would it seem, I wondered, seeing him out of context? How would either of us feel for that matter, used to the ragged wild times in old clothes. Would he be wearing a pinstripe suit, would it fit? Georgette used to complain that he didn't even own a shirt (or only one) and borrowed his father's rather ill-fitting jackets when he applied for a job interview. . . . he spent the summer in faded T-shirts and jeans . . . Of course he did, that was the summer when he had a job as a gardener, and rebuilt our wall with us.

When I reached the café where we had arranged to meet he was already there, finishing his lunch. We both laughed, there was a joke in it somewhere. A long talk ensued about the details, whether S.A.F.E.R. would buy it if he could not get there first. The owner was one of four brothers who had quarrelled and all wanted to leave, they had moved out a year ago; this was why it was for sale. They each owned a share and different lots of land – so four smallholders to be sorted out by a *notaire* – entirely possible if someone could just produce the missing £70,000 far below the true value, since the wine was *appellation contrôlée* and there would be other produce.

We agreed to meet again two weeks later sur place at the *domaine*, near Gordes, near Roussillon, when he would be back from Lille.

He had not worn a pinstripe suit, just an open shirt, very neat, clean jeans and a blazer. A coat over his shoulder flew out in a swinging movement as I watched him walk off fast, completely at home in Paris.

The plan was that Marc would drive to his parents' house in the hamlet near Beaumont – a three hour drive from his present job – that I would meet him there and we would spend the night, then go the next morning, another hour's drive south, to visit the site.

It was a bleak day towards the end of February 1986 when I drove over the small mountain road through Dieulefit and Ste Jalle, coming down from the north through the Drôme and over the Col d'Ey into Buis-les-Baronnies. I stopped on the corner after the Col, where the road turns to descend, to look at the memorial stone, as I always did.

> *Du sommet de cette montagne Olivier Bourles 31 ans*
> *Libériste*
> *Partie pour l'Eternité*
> *Emporté par le vent*
> *22 mai 1983*

The term *libériste* was odd. It is not in the dictionary. What was meant exactly? At first I used to think it might have been an exalted suicide. A flight to some sort of freedom. Who was he "liberating"? Himself ? The world? It remained an enigma. Since it was still early I decided to go to the *mairie* in Buis to find out about the young man who had left for eternity carried by the wind . . .

The drive down the precipitous corniche road was unfriendly, the weather and the season were a dun, grey colour, no new leaves growing – it was lonely and also, though not actually hostile, unamiable – except for the isolated farm towards the end of the descent where I stopped to buy olive oil (straight from their orchard, the most pure available).

In the *mairie* they were uninterested in the young man who had lost his life. No one had enquired about him before; it was evidently an interruption of their routine. A *gendarme* who happened to be there informed me he had been a hang glider, his body had never been found. Usually deaths are registered, but perhaps if there was no body . . . No one knew where he came from, no one cared apparently, except whoever wrote the epitaph, who indeed seemed tragically bereft.

I was glad to leave Buis. In winter it is itself at least, no crowds, even quite empty – a beautiful, small town; yet there is something depressing, perhaps almost bad about the place. Even the mountains have sinister names: Montagne de Linceuil (shroud) and Piégon (a trap). The only friendly people were those of the restaurant Bontempelli where the black olives were so exceedingly delicious I could have made a meal of nothing else.

Vaison-la-Romaine, by contrast, was full of vitality and jollity. Perhaps Buis has been killed by tourism and has no soul left, whereas Vaison, where tourists also abound, has kept its own, important local life. This could be the reason the people of Buis are so anti-outsider – whether me, any traveller, or a dead young man who loved their mountains . . . Love is not enough without belonging, there is a collective resentment.

The road to Malaucène was drab, the Ventoux was not showing, clouds were so thick over it there could well have been nothing there at all. There is now a rubbish dump just before the entrance to Malaucéne, but once inside the *mail* the little town can be counted on to be its plain, unpretentious self. The road out to Beaumont also looked drab, with some litter on the fields, the land naked and muddy, not camouflaged by summer growth. When I reached the Paganin house, however, there was a friendly welcome, the dogs did not bark and a fire was burning.

Jean-Louis was out by the road digging up the first *pissenlit* with his knife. For dinner we had soup of haricot beans and barley, then two *patés* that Georgette had made, one of hare, the other of thrush, eaten with the *pissenlit* salad (Jean-Louis complaining that she had not done this salad traditionally with bacon), then cheese and a *crème caramel*. I had brought wine from Tain l'Hermitage on the way down, the Collines Rhodaniennes *vin du pays*, and whisky for Jean-Louis. They had been to visit Marc's *domaine*. Georgette seemed receptive to the idea, but Jean-Louis was against it. He admired Marc's present opportunity and could not conceive of wanting to throw up such a safe job for a gamble. We discussed what investment would be needed before it could produce; new vine stock is 5 or 6 francs a plant, to replant 10 hectares would cost about £3,000. Jean-Louis had carefully estimated that only half the vines needed replanting. We talked of crops in general, walnuts in Isére, politicians, Thatcher whom he greatly admires. (The previous summer a workman in a bar in Estremadura was equally enthusiastic about her – all through Europe I have noticed she appeals to labourers.)[13]

Headlights outside announced Marc's late arrival and caused a skirmish amongst the dogs. We drank *tisane de tilleul* after dinner and the atmosphere changed. Georgette remained in her chair with the cat on her shoulder, Marc stood by the fire looking taller and leaner than when we first knew him – and there was a feeling of antagonism between him and his father. Marc does not want to be a "salary-earner" all his life and says so with vehemence. Georgette understands. On one of our walks together, years before, I remember her saying, "It is important to have castles in Spain even if they do not come about. Jean-Louis thinks this foolish . . ." She understood, but perhaps did not believe that this plan would work.

"I need space," Marc said, after they had talked heatedly of his brothers, what he considered the boredom of their life, also his father's past life and beginnings. He was scornful that before meeting Georgette Jean-Louis had been a salesman, though he had now learned to be one himself. How could he save on 6,000 francs a month? And in the last year he had only had a two-day holiday . . .

(When he visited his parents he usually combined it with business, *en route* somewhere with cases of wine.) Under the surface he was angry. Jean-Louis lay back on the sofa after his whisky and his good dinner and teased his son. He was no longer anxious about him, and had decided to write off the problem. He just wanted him to be safe, but never mind; and for both safety and his father Marc felt disdain.

[13] He was lamenting the strike of the vine-growers and much else. I pointed out that we also had strikes – perhaps the worst of anywhere. "Ah – but you have la Tatzher," he said with feeling.

In my bedroom there were lace curtains made of thick white cotton crocheted in small squares with a pattern of wheat sheaves at the bottom making a wide hem; the bedspread was also crocheted, but with another pattern. These had been made by Madame Plantevin. It was very cold, and it seemed strange to be sleeping in their house.

In the morning, coffee by the fire that was still warm and had been rekindled, then Marc and I set off in two cars, since after the visit we were each to take different roads. Georgette, always unruffled and amused, said to me, "On Marc's last visit he spent four days here and we never exchanged a word."

When we passed by the Plantevin house, the old man was already out fishing rather hopelessly under the small bridge. Marc stopped and leapt out to see him, and they had a brief conversation about the fact that there were no fish. "So you're off to the *domaine!*" said the old man, looking at me with twinkling eyes, as if pleased at some plot. Marc hugged him with an eagerness he had not shown at home.

South from Carpentras and Venasque the road crosses astonishing countryside; Marc finds it more beautiful than his parents' area. It is large and grand, also well-kept and clean. Marc says this is because most of it belongs to foreigners, which he does not resent, as his father would. (Surely there must also be local farmers? Marc has rather taken against his home region, for the moment at least.) After the village of Murs a huge panorama opens. In summer there are many tourists, centred at Gordes, where in the Renaissance château (built onto a twelfth century fortress) there is a permanent exhibition of Vasarely, and below the town a settlement of ancient abodes like stone beehives, called *bories*. Perhaps the charm of Ste Marguerite and our valleys is that they are still secret and fairly private, but the southern Vaucluse is more sensational.

We walked all over his land, already calling it "his", though he frequently referred to it as "ours". We inspected which vineyards would need replanting and which only pruning. There is a large, empty field which could have any sort of crop – a track leading uphill to the highest point of the property, in a pine wood, through which there is a view of Roussillon, a village so called because it is made of the bright red stone of the cliffs around it. It appears to grow out of these cliffs, all the same incredible colour, scarlet or beetroot according to the light and time of day. The Ventoux sits to the right of this view, looking widespread from here, as if relaxed and comfortable – covered with thick snow in the cold winter. Marc talked enthusiastically and kept questioning to know what I thought. Wheat could be planted in the empty field . . . *grenache* grapes . . . *carignan* . . . *syrah* . . . in two years it could all bear fruit. To restore the houses would be expensive. Marc is also a mason, he eagerly undertook the idea of doing everything – he had two unemployed friends who were hard workers, he could bring them here.

Rain started as we went down the track – soft at first but becoming penetrating – and our shoes were caked with reddish yellow mud. Where would the money come from? £120,000 does not seem much for one hundred acres and four houses; if an agent flaired it the figure would triple. The houses are not beautiful *mas provençal*, but are made of good large stones, *pierres de taille*, and have little archways and steps. Two of them have telephones and are habitable. The idea of a room anywhere in Provence, with jasmine outside and a distant squawking of poultry (as in Billeul's almond orchard) – seemed peaceful. But now as the rain ceased the *mistral* rose, lashing at us in gusts of wet cold, seeming to dampen the plan, or to warn: it might be rough. Neither of us could wait two years until the crops grew with no income.

We got into Marc's car and sat huddled together in it, sheltered under a big barn roof, shivering, talking, both understanding what had to be done and seeing how it could be so easy. Inside the car became gradually warm and alive with excitement and our belief in this venture, planning who would have which house – only lacking the backer. We also talked of this book and his part in it. When I had first written to tell him and ask for approval, he had answered: "*Bien sur, d'accord – être dans un bouquin pour la posterité, c'est exaltant! Ma modestie en prend un coup.*" I asked him whether, when the time came, he thought Jean-Louis was likely to object to it being in print that he hated the mayor. "He doesn't care who knows or what anyone thinks," Marc said of his father. Here lies the man's honesty and strength; he may well have *antipathies*, but makes no pretence to hide them and knows no hypocrisy. The hatreds of the Provençal people can be said to have a certain grace, like some old ritual dance. Jean-Louis, in spite of his rages, is a good man – his animosity is harmless, like a game.

Before we drove away, each in our different cars, he stood by the window of mine, lingering, repeating what we knew – as if it surely could not be finished. . . . . I thought he would be cold in his soaked leather jacket and put my hand against his cheek and said to take care.

. . . His head is rather small on a long body, like a puma, his face has a quality of being completely alive, missing nothing – a quick immediate grasp, the laugh. Not the least part of this investment for the backer would be Marc himself, with his Brevet T.S.O. and his knowledge.

"If it doesn't work," he then said, "I'll drive with you to Turkey." (I had told him I might drive across Europe in September.) "I'll leave anyway. Maybe Paraguay after all."

"Is there still a plan?"

"No. Yes, but alone. Not the man. He has found a job as night watchman of a factory, he says he will never travel again now, anywhere. He was in the Foreign Legion, he's seen enough; it's as if overnight he grew old. But Paraguay is still there; it's a desert, there are hardly any people."

I thought: if it doesn't work, why not Australia? He doesn't speak English, but could learn. I have cousins there who own a vineyard – I could write to them. It was true he was no *salarier*, he needed an outlet, he had a potential almost of greatness, but if disappointed he might turn into a wastrel. There was a sort of despair in his longing for what was not, after all a dangerous idea, but feasible and positive – only just out of reach. The *mistral* swirled round us now as if it would tear up the vines by the roots before Marc could claim them.

We left each other in frustration, something had only just begun. I said I would come back. "And don't be in a hurry!" he made me promise, and we laughed. As I drove away toward Avignon I saw him in the rear mirror, standing at the crossroads. I had somehow become identified with, and muddled into, his hope; the idea of his own land, "our" village; for one second he looked like someone's old lover left there; but then he turned and jumped into his car and both of us were gone, down our different roads.

★   ★   ★

A traveller might find the following hotels in the vicinity useful: the family-run Beffroi in Vaison in the *haute ville* is small and charming, with Provençal furniture in its rooms. It has a garden on a terrace with a view, rare in medieval towns which were built against sieges and enclosed for protection. Dark, narrow streets can seem grim, but the *haute ville* is full of flowers, and the land grows wild towards the ruined castle at the top. There is a fountain opposite the front door of the hotel.[14] The dining room is in a courtyard surrounded by fig trees, and the food is excellent. The approach is up a cobbled street, where parking is difficult; best to leave the car on the esplanade outside this old part of town.

In Seguret, the Table du Comtat, at the end of the range of Montmirail mountains, sits in the last jagged steps facing a long view across an infinite plain, so contrastingly flat that sometimes, when blue and misty, it looks like the sea. There is good food and a small pool. On Christmas Eve there is a Provençal vigil.

In Avignon, Le Vernet (restaurant only, no rooms) is in the centre of the district of museums and shops – it is set in an oasis of palm trees and green plants. On a sultry day (Avignon can be suffocating) there is no coolness comparable to the dark shade of thick leaves.

In Montfavet, a suburb of Avignon, there is Les Frènes, which is useful after the museum visits are over, for its swimming pool. Though in an area of dusty main roads, it is in a side lane and has a luxuriant garden; tables are set on a flowery terrace, food is subtle and original, raw fish salad a speciality.

Near Orange, and slightly pompous, is the Château de Rochegude. The village of Rochegude is quiet and entirely as it always was, with fields starting immediately outside with no transition, its calm life unaffected by the hotel. The château has courtyards with statues, a fountain, and a very large swimming pool reached across a bridge that spans a village street, and through a park. It is in a romantic setting of lawns, pine trees and cork oak, and at the far end of the blue water is a terrace with Italianate balustrades. Inside the hotel the decoration has obviously been conceived by a different person. It is furnished with flamboyant vulgarity, but is very comfortable. This hotel is useful to know after a tiring trip on the motorway as it is near the exit at Bollène[15] but its presence could not be guessed. Rochegude feels far from anywhere.

---

[14] Fountains are a special feature of Provence. Since the climate is so hot and dry, it might be thought that water should be used sparingly, as in Andalusia or Australia – but here it runs in plenty everywhere because there are underground streams, thanks to which every village has its fountain. In the white-hot summers there is always a sound of splashing water, and many fountains are encircled with dripping ferns.

[15] A good Provençal non-tourist town. The municipal museum has interesting local drawings, also some by Picasso and Chagall.

Spending a night there once in a single, small room, I looked out of the window rather late at the miles of vineyards under a low orange moon – the only noise was the crickets – and there was that ancient quiet that comes out of the earth at night when the sounds of the busy world have ceased: an awareness of eternity I had so often felt in our Provençal home.

Monsieur Billeul's farm seen from our terrace

Epilogue

At a greengrocer's in the north, "What kind of grapes are these?"
"Seedless."

Two girls on a London bus: "Where did you go for your holiday?"
"Palma."

"Where's that?"

"Don't know, I went on an aeroplane."

On the herb-and-spice shelf in a shop: microwave seasoning. Also microwave browning (? for unnatural ovens then . . .)

A funny-sad world, where the sense of basic origins has been lost.

This book is not meant to be a lament for the passing of Europe, though there is room for nostalgia – but tries to preserve something precious. It is not change that is wrong – there has always been change – but its rapidity. An eighteenth-century house beside a petrol station . . .

Until the last war, change used to be evolution, not shock, so it did not jar. It grew like a graft on a plant, out of the very ancient roots of Europe, out of its past as it always had for centuries.

There may be a new (possibly federal) Europe coming as the old frontiers start to lose their rigidity. The absence of war for a long period is allowing the regions to grow again – it is safe, neighbouring countries no longer fight. There is hope that the identity of each area may be able to develop – in which case the regions are not lost, but found.

But for that which has gone . . . here is simply a souvenir.

Afterthought

Dinner in the Dróme

". . . and then I started the game of imagining their talk, overheard in a café, or more likely in their kitchen. After that I sometimes 'went to dinner in the Dróme'. It was my escape game."

SHE
Don't you say good evening to Bernard any more?

HE
He eats robins.

SHE
Only once, because he found one fallen.

HE
He grills little birds on spits. And makes thrush pâté.

SHE
You eat thrush too, so does everyone here, it's delicious. In Italy they eat little birds, ucelli . . .

HE
I can't really get chummy with a man who eats robins for Chrissake.

SHE
The thrushes here migrate anyway, they aren't like ours.

HE

Not surprising. If I were a thrush I wouldn't come here at all.

SHE

You came here to live because you wanted to be a peasant. Close to the earth, forget the cities and lead poisoning petrol and the strikes . . . W ell that's what peasants do, they eat robins, they don't give a bugger about the view. Never notice. See it all their lives anyway, so what's new about it? Think city people like us gurgling at the sunset are freaks.

HE

You mean even in Saou? With that huge boulder right in the middle of the street, you tell me they don't notice it's different when they go to the town to market?

SHE

Oh . . . I don't tell you anything. It took hundreds of years to make civilisation, thousands even. Houses different in each region according to weather, crops and the local materials . . . thatched roofs in Brittany with iris growing along the top to hold the join . . . Roman tiles here . . . and now since the war all the same cement everywhere. Fast food and concrete blocks. Less here than anywhere else, but beginning here too. They can't notice or they wouldn't build their ugly new villas the minute they get any money.

HE

Yes. And dogs. Take dogs. I don't like all dogs any more than I like all people. This man Bernard, he won't hear a word against dogs, even when his tore my coat. No apology. Dear little chap. It gets me. Snacks at the table, licks everything. Can't have dinner with Bernard and Josette without their bloody dog swiping what's on your plate . . . Repulsivo.

SHE

Just because you haven't got a dog any more.

HE

But when I had dogs they were trained. I gave up because of trips back to England and the quarantine, but since we don't go any more . . . If we stay here we'll have a dog and it will be different.

SHE

What do you mean, if we stay here? We've been here fifteen years.

HE

But only here. Not going away. Not leaving the dog behind. He will be sleek and look forward to his own star dinner in his own bowl, and watch us eat ours, happy like a proper English dog, not hanging round the table like a beggar and longing – and taught to long – for snacks, like a city kid longs for a fix. Never really satisfied, then finally dies of cirrhosis.

SHE

You get so excited about everything here. Still, after so long.

HE

It's my nature. I got as excited over you when we met.

SHE

And now, fifteen years later, this village still . . . and not me?

HE

If you look at me like that. Always. We ran away together. I gave it all up for you. It's just gone in deeper. I can't leap about after twenty years . . . but if a chap eats robins, I leap.

SHE

It was only one robin for God's sake and it was dead anyway. Why do you have to go on and on.

HE

He eats finches too. Regularly. Nets them, which is not sporting. Shoots all the time too. Has to kill.

SHE

So do we in England. Thousands of grouse. Repulsivo.

HE

At least it's organised. The woods are stocked with pheasants. At nesting time we stop. That's fair.

SHE

They stop here too, they have their season.

HE

Not really, they just pretend.

SHE

Nothing's fair anyway. It's still killing, wherever it happens. You came here to get away from 'Ban The Bomb' and you're founding 'Ban The Robin-Eaters'.

HE

I believe in banning the bomb. But not the processions and flag-waving that don't achieve anything. It's really very important, though, not to eat robins. The bomb is too big for me, I can't cope. There should be a better way to stop it than barricades. And nuclear power. What happens to the waste? They bury atomic waste. So how long before it explodes, or there is no more room? Ostrich – head in sand, just keep burying what you don't like. Man doesn't even have an animal's common sense. And so petty . . . All against everything now. Why aren't any of them for something? Hey, must we have your tights and knickers hanging everywhere round this room? I just noticed.

SHE

They were drying on the line in the sun and mistral *and getting that wind-dried smell, then the wind dropped and it rained so I brought them in.*

HE

So now they'll get that wonderful woods smoke smell in here by the fire.

SHE

You wanted to live like a peasant.

HE

So I sit festooned with knickers at dinner.

SHE

Let's hang that sour bacon on the fig tree tomorrow for the blue tits, it's cold lately.

HE

What about the cats? They've all got balls in this village that's another thing, not one is neutered so there are a hundred cats in a hamlet of nine houses. No one owns or feeds them. Good luck with your bacon, you'll just lure the birds for cats' targets. Since when do you eat dinner with your glasses on? You've never done so before.

SHE

I'm tired. Maybe I grew old when you weren't looking. I realise I do see the food better with them on.

HE

This is delicious. What is it?

SHE

Roast robin.

HE

Please?

SHE

It's the pork from yesterday ground through the mouli *with thyme and garlic and parsley and scooped out aubergine, then put back inside the aubergine and baked in a pudding tin. You turn it out like a black cake.*

HE

So the black outside is the skin? People don't usually eat the skin.

SHE

They do here. It's a local recipe, a Comtat dish. Remember the home-heated factory food in English pubs? You wanted away from that too. Though according to the magazines it has improved – gone the other way – they write about food all the time now.

HE

Peace. That's all a man anywhere wants. His dinner, his woman, a patch of land, a view if possible, left alone to do his own thing, and freedom of choice ...

SHE

A bit more ... Stars and flowers.

HE

So why do men fight when they all want the same thing?

SHE

That's why. They want each other's.

HE

Bombs through the ministry window the other day, to demonstrate for peace – what a farce. Violence for peace. Terrorists in name of religion. Though I suppose there always were religious wars – but the fighting was between those involved, not just any chap quite outside, travelling home to see his family, nothing to do with the feuds. Now you've got that huge iron hammer holding up your knickers over the fireplace! Hot diggity, smoked undies.

SHE

They weren't going to dry so far away. The clothes can stay in the kitchen all night while the fire dies down. Listen, you have no ambition any more.

HE

Ambition? After Oxford and Chicago University ... I liked editing the magazine ... I came here as a failed writer pretending all I needed was time to write. I'm so busy hacking brambles and sawing logs, I've got an excuse not to do anything about it. What would I write actually? It's all been written. I just want to sit here and see the beauty before Europe is all built over. Our south-west view like Tuscany, yet more remote. Unknown northern Provence, somewhere in the Drôme. Maybe that is not much of an ambition. Maybe you are right ... I'm negative and stuck.

SHE

Here's the new neighbour, he's just outside.

HE
Oh, no, not now. Tell him I'm ill. Or pissed. Or a shitbag at heart who doesn't like people, doesn't want to know anyone new. A misanthrope.

NEIGHBOUR
Bonsoir Monsieur-Dame.

SHE
Mon mari est fatigué. Ce serait mieux demain. *He's gone.*

HE
Well done. That was quick. He's a good chap, he got the message fast. What did he want anyway?

SHE
Probably about the right of way across our field.

HE
Field you call it! We've only got a few thousand square metres and he has to cross it all the time.

SHE
You knew when you came here to collect logs from his wood on the other side. Fine by me. Nice to see him. Picturesque. But I didn't know he would clear the wood and build a hideous urban villa, not even in local stone, a flaunting eyesore, and then make it over to his son who would drive to it in a smelly car, leaving the car parked to block the view. Suddenly we are in the suburbs. Might as well be in the outskirts of Marseilles. Might even be better, we could go to the movies. Can't one ever be left alone? You get a good thing going, then someone has to spoil it.

SHE
That's politics. Anyway we tried for the wood, but they wouldn't sell.

HE
So let him pass and get used to it? Legally I have to, I suppose. But I wish he still had a horse. Glad to see a horse any time. I'll never get used to his car. Or his appearance, a fat city slob. The old man was different . . . what a face, bony,

weathered, they don't come like that any more. Never guessed the mayor would give him a building permit.

SHE

We'll have to move perhaps. We could see the notaire and ask what's going. Now we have learned about Napoleonic law and the patchwork land arrangements, we could be cleverer. Dearest, I know you didn't really want to leave England.

HE

Yes I did. I was fed up with the stagnation and the boredom of the on-and-on politics. But if we have to move again . . . well, I suppose somewhere else down here . . . I like the cubist villages with ruined castles on their tops, the wine and weather and good sense, lavender and apricots – whatever their civilisation is made of. I'm not unpatriotic, but I don't like what England has become. I did want to leave, don't worry. I suppose I would go back to fight if there were a war, except it would not be that sort of war any more.

SHE

All the same, don't think I don't understand. You can like it here, but still be nostalgic. For the good English things, or what England was. Or even just your old friends, specially your old friends. That day long ago when we first became residents here, and the car plates were changed to twenty-six for the Drôme – whereas I had been longing to be a local and belong here, not the outsider, the tourist, les anglais . . . I saw you putting our English car plates away carefully with your old photographs in the attic – and I knew. You didn't throw them out with the rubbish, you kept them.

HE

Next Christmas we'll send cards with traditional robins on them but they'll be in pie dishes.

SHE

I do understand.

HE

But I'm not sad. Life is nostalgic anyway, even if you spend it all in one village. You grow old, you change, you remember. It's lucky the people here are so nice.

Bernard, apart from killing all the birds, is good company. And helpful with jobs. He even understands my French. They seem to like us – or respect that this is our only home. We aren't like the Parisians with holiday homes south of here, who are viewed with scorn. All the rest of France seems to hate Parisians. Maybe I am a bit homesick at times, but it's for the past. If I went back I wouldn't find the thing I missed. Occasionally though, I do wonder . . . if you die first, what would I do here? I don't even speak the language properly.

SHE
It's the same for me. If you die first, even though I do speak the language, what good would that do if I never have anything to say again? Except that I miss him, I miss him, he was part of me, how can I survive?

HE
For God's sake . . . don't cry now baby, we aren't dead yet – it's this wine. Too much twelve degrees. Blow your nose. That's better, laugh and cry at the same time . . . I'd be a foreigner if I went back to England now, I've been gone too long. Listen: let's not think of this. It's going to happen. We know. So let's have now – that's what we've got: now. Our life is whittled down somehow, we should have expanded it in middle age. Don't laugh at my belly, that's corny, I mean it. Our ideas. The people we don't see. We should make an effort.

SHE
Why see bores? I don't agree. We've pruned our life and don't want to see bores any more. All that rushing about imagining we were being kind and useful – it was nonsense.

HE
They weren't all bores.

SHE
Of course not, lovely friends. But we're talking about all the other people, social gatherings, duties . . .

HE
Maybe it's selfish.

SHE

So let's be selfish. And we aren't. We still have some lame-duck regulars. I believe in seeing the result. Do-goodery is only guilt. Hypocritical. We do expand anyway – we read and think – It took enough trouble getting here, we've earned it – we are free . . .

HE

We aren't merely looking at butterflies through a lens like Nabokov?

SHE

Nothing wrong with that, if we are.

HE

We sit here in rocking chairs while the world explodes . . . as if we don't hear the noise.

SHE

What's the good of hearing? We can't stop it. But I do often think of Jimmy and wonder what he might be doing.

HE

Why think of him? It's useless. He wouldn't have helped the world, he didn't want to be in it. What's he got to do with pruning our life? That part was pruned for us. Just accept.

SHE

He was our son wasn't he? Why did he have to go on that Himalayan expedition?

HE

He found the world dull and wanted to climb the peaks. But when he reached them the view wasn't showing. W here's the coffee? I don't want to talk of Jimmy. Is there a dessert? If I had the choice, somewhere floating in the universe or ether before I was born, I would say to my parents: don't have me – once I'm here, I'm stuck.

SHE

It's the fashion to be negative.

HE

Obviously. Too many people for each job, too many factories, population growing like locusts, but no politician will say there will always be unemployment, they funk it. How can there ever be enough jobs for all the people, and machines making man unnecessary? And no wonder the food is hormone and chemically grown – how can there be enough otherwise for the hordes? Package tours dumping people down who don't know where they are. What's it called here? they ask. Don't know, some place the travel agency said was a good deal. Bingo on the beach at Benidorm. Or how to ruin Cyprus, all included for £200. Package tours should just be to help people who want to go somewhere, but not to dump down slobs who don't care.

SHE

Darling. I can put up with anything as long as you are there. Forever or never, if you're with me – but if not . . .

HE

Thank you.

SHE

What for? I'm just a coward.

HE

No, you're full of love.

SHE

This is tremendous, after twenty years . . .

HE

Where's the dessert, what is it?

SHE

Summer pudding.

HE

In winter?

SHE

I cheated a little. Remains of some bottled plums – call it early spring pudding, the winter's nearly over.

HE

Oh Lord, here's that whizzy cat just come in.

SHE

He's beautiful. Scrape off your plate for him.

HE

He won't eat aubergine.

SHE

He'll eat anything.

HE

Prefers robins.

SHE

Here pussy, minou, minou . . .

HE

There he goes trembling his tail and stinking the place out. He's a whizzer cat I tell you. There isn't a cat in this village who isn't a wild, unhouse-trained scavenger. Throw him out. He's beautiful, but he pees like a fox.

SHE

It isn't pee, it's pleasure, anyway foxes don't do that.

HE

Then let's have a fox – except they have rabies here.

SHE

Here's Bernard's dog now, come for a snack – all because I left the door open when I went out to the larder.

HE

Throw them all out for God's sake and shut the door.

SHE

Now it's quiet. Did you see that spark? Look it's caught in the chimney like a star. How will I find you in the next world if you don't believe? We won't wake up in the same place.

HE

It's all rot. We won't wake up anywhere, we don't go on, there isn't a next world.

SHE

Then who is the fifth Marx brother who triggered it all off? What is the point?

HE

This is not a useful conversation.

SHE

Faith has nothing to do with intelligence. You have it or you don't.

HE

Well I don't.

SHE

You can't reason it. But if there is something . . . I'll have to search for you and drag you there.

HE

There is no future in this conversation, I say. Today the brambles came up easily, digging was a pleasure, because of our SKB last autumn and then our fire. Quite exciting, wasn't it, finding such good earth underneath? We've been sitting here all these years saying there was nothing but stones round the house, nothing would grow except hollyhocks and that old fig tree that's been here a hundred years with its roots all through the wall, but no place to plant anything new – you hit rock three inches down – and then bang . . . ! In the right of way you call our field, in the corner we called the bad patch, under the brambles and ancient rusty cans ... suddenly today up come the roots and there is our soil ... Not spoilt with fertilizers – just twenty-year-old donkey dung and deep earth – and one old rose. The endurance of the eternal rose ... We can really grow things now: lettuces of all different types, broad beans ...

SHE
Until fallout covers the world.

HE
Now you're the one who's negative. Don't think of that, there's no point, anyway maybe it won't happen, there might be a miraculous awakening. We have to go on, so ignore it.

SHE
Why did we ignore that patch so long?

HE
Because I never thought we could clear it ourselves. Thought I'd have to hire a man with a machine, and would not find one willing for such a small job – they're better paid to do big things. I used to scratch away at it – but you're right – we were fools not to do it before.

SHE
Do you think you see in the next world? I mean how does one recognise a person? Do you feel them?

HE
Stop it. I'm glad I'm not God with the homework he will have to do. I am content to just stop. Only not yet.

SHE
But I'll miss you.

HE
Soon I'll hit you. If we haven't agreed on this subject for twenty years, we won't now.

SHE

Revelations happen. Miracles also, you just said so.

HE

The almond trees will blossom next month in all the valleys. We won't need the fire, the log chore will be over. I'll plant the seeds. What a climate. Did you notice the clear light today after the rain? That special winter light of Provence.

SHE

Haute Provence.

HE

Did you see the light?

SHE

Of course. And was gulping and breathing clear air all day. I'll never grow blasé. And that smell of crushed fennel when you are weeding. The bad weather lasts just long enough to fool you ... "could it be set in?" Then the same afternoon the little blue hills come back out of the mist into the sunlight ... It is never a bore like steady, even heat in the desert.

HE

I never knew you'd lived in the desert.

SHE

Steady English drizzle if you prefer. It isn't monotonous. Good weather but continual changes.

HE

That's why Cezanne liked it. The light.

SHE

He was much further south. Will you love me when I'm ninety?

HE

No because I won't be here. I wonder if those old iris roots got burned or if they'll survive.

SHE

People invent plots. In a play, something has to happen. What I like here is that nothing happens. Please let nothing happen, so we can just go on like this.

HE

Something will happen one day. It will end.

SHE

I don't want to know about that. I wish I were an animal, they don't know.

HE

Animalito *darling. Or is it* animalita?

SHE

And yet we should know, so as to appreciate. It is so rare, so simple, yet so hard to find. All we count on is each other, to have and to hold, as long as . . .

HE

For Chrissake. Anyway Bernard does like the eagle, I'll give him that. He would never shoot the eagle.

SHE

Yes. And when the pair fly over, he runs to fetch you every time, so you can see them soar; but they don't come very often, do they. . .

HE

Just hold my hand now. Let's sit quietly by the fire and not talk any more. Actually things do happen, not one season is ever the same as the year before. It's the rhythm, I suppose, that doesn't change. So let it be the same tomorrow, year after year, season after season . . . just let it stay the same . . .

About the Author

Gael Elton Mayo (1923-92) was the youngest daughter of a pioneering, Australian-born professor of industrial psychology at Harvard. She married a white Russian during World War Two, when she was seventeen, and nearly died of puerperal fever after giving birth to their son during the bombardment of Bordeaux. They eventually escaped from war-torn France. Her first novel was published by Doubleday, New York, when she was twenty. As a writer she had five more novels published and three volumes of autobiography & memoir; as a painter she had nine exhibitions; and as a singer-songwriter she appeared on TV. She endured numerous facial cancer operations in the later years of her life.

www.bookblast.com

Other books by the same author

Non Fiction
  The Mad Mosaic
  Living with Beelzebub

Fiction
  Honeymoon in Hell
  The Devil and the Fool
  Nobody's Nothing
  Last Seen Near Trafalgar
  It's Locked in with You
  Undertow

Gael Elton Mayo in 1992 © BookBlast Ltd

CPSIA information can be obtained
at www.ICGtesting.com
Printed in the USA
LVHW081431141020
668800LV00036B/1593